HEAVEN ON EARTH

Capturing Jonathan Edwards's Vision of Living in Between

STEPHEN J. NICHOLS

CROSSWAY BOOKS

A PUBLISHING MINISTRY OF
GOOD NEWS PUBLISHERS
WHEATON, ILLINOIS

Heaven on Earth

Copyright © 2006 by Stephen J. Nichols

Published by Crossway Books
    A publishing ministry of Good News Publishers
    1300 Crescent Street
    Wheaton, Illinois 60187

Cover design: Jon McGrath

Cover photo: Getty Images

First printing, 2006

Printed in the United States of America

Library of Congress Cataloging-in-Publication Data
Nichols, Stephen J., 1970–
   Heaven on earth : capturing Jonathan Edwards' vision of living in between / Stephen J. Nichols.
     p. cm.
   Includes bibliographical references.
   ISBN 13: 978-1-58134-785-2
   ISBN 10: 1-58134-785-5 (tpb)
    1. Edwards, Jonathan, 1703–1758. 2. Congregational
churches—Sermons. 3. Sermons, American—18th century.
   I. Edwards, Jonathan 1703–1758. I. Title
BX7260.E3N528   2006
230'.58092—dc22   2006011637

ML		15	14	13	12	11	10	09	08	07	06
14	13	12	11	10	9	8	7	6	5	4	3	2	1

For
Keith and Beverly Haselhorst,
relatives by law, friends by choice,
with grateful appreciation

CONTENTS

ACKNOWLEDGMENTS

IT IS MY PLEASURE to thank those who contributed to this book. I am grateful to Justin Taylor for his encouragement of the project and for reading early drafts. Dale Mort read every word of the manuscript, offering invaluable suggestions. The finished product is much improved thanks to his keen eye and input. I am also grateful to the administrators and the faculty development committee at Lancaster Bible College for encouraging my writing and for granting a sabbatical. Al Fisher and his team at Crossway made the journey from idea to manuscript to book a most gratifying one.

My wife, Heidi, once again offered unstinting support. She is a kind and careful editor and proofreader, every writer's dream. Her parents, Keith and Beverly Haselhorst, also chipped in, offering input on early drafts. They model the principles within this book, making it quite fitting for me to dedicate it to them.

INTRODUCTION

How to Read an Edwards Sermon

IN HEAVEN WE WILL enjoy perfect, unbroken fellowship with the Triune God. We will relish the glory of God. We will savor the sweetness of Christ. We will have perfect fellowship with the Holy Spirit. Why not start now?

In heaven, bickering, complaining, and acts of injustice will all have fallen away. Peace and harmony and justice will be the order. We will love God perfectly. We will even love all our brothers and sisters in Christ perfectly. So why not begin now? There's no reason not to. In fact, there's every reason in the world to do so.

C. S. Lewis once said, "If you read history you will find that the Christians who did the most for the present world were precisely those who thought most of the next." And one of those Christians was certainly Jonathan Edwards. We learn from Edwards that heaven isn't only about the future. It has everything to do with life on earth, life in between. He reminds us of our duty to live on earth in light of heaven and to endeavor to bring the realities and the beauty of heaven to earth—even if only in miniature.

Just about anywhere you look in the writings of Jonathan Edwards, you bump into his thoughts on heaven and how those thoughts should make a difference in our lives. In the chapters to follow, I have selected a handful of sermons for our focus from the mountain of literature. These sermons inspire and instruct. They inspire us as they brilliantly display Edwards's contagious vision of the glory of heaven. And they instruct by clearly and convincingly teaching us how to live in between our coming to Christ and our going home to heaven.

Jonathan Edwards's sermons are readable and applicable to contemporary audiences. They are, nevertheless, from a different era, the Puritan era—a time when the sermon was king. Puritans expected much of their preachers, and the preachers expected much of their congregations. One of the ways that we can get in on this as well is to understand the structure of these Puritan sermons.

All Puritan sermons look alike. They have three components:

- Text
- Doctrine
- Application

They started with a biblical text, usually just a verse or a short portion of Scripture. They mostly, though not always, followed the reading of the text with a brief exposition. Next came the doctrine. This was declared in a single sentence and was then developed for many paragraphs in detailed outlines. One doctrine could yield anywhere from two to five and many times more main points. These main points often had multiple sub-points. Preaching was taken very seriously and was considered worthy of exhausting labor.

They closed with the application, what they called the "Use," as in "what *use* is this doctrine to me?" or "Improvement," as in "how does this doctrine *improve* my life?" Often the application portion was as long as the doctrine portion. It too could have numerous major points and sub-points. Sometimes the first part of the sermon would be preached in the morning, and the application section would be preached in the afternoon.

You find this structure in just about every Edwards sermon. In the following chapters I'll refer to a sermon's "doctrine" or "application," reflecting this structure that Edwards used in his sermons.

Being aware of this structure, which is unlike most sermons today, helps in reading Edwards's sermons. It also helps if we know something about Edwards's approach to the Christian life. One way to describe Edwards sees him emphasizing mind and heart together. Actually, it might be better to say mind and heart together *and on fire*. Edwards, when he spoke of the Triune God, used words like *relish, savor, enjoy,* and *desire* alongside a vocabulary of *know, understand,* and *contemplate.* He was a rare example of this dangerous (in a good way) combination. This too will surface in the following chapters.

Finally, Edwards would likely blush at all the attention he keeps on receiving. He's a good guide for us only because he so well points to Scripture and to Christ and then quickly steps aside. In my own thinking of the Christian life, life in between the hope of heaven and the realization of heaven, I have found Edwards to be a sound, provocative, and deft guide. But he's not the ultimate guide.

The author of Hebrews has a great deal to say about living the Christian life. The author even uses men and women from the past to spur us on as we make our journey through this world to the better country of heaven (Hebrews 11). But then the author holds out for us the ultimate example, calling us to look to Jesus, "the founder and perfecter of our faith" (Heb. 12:2). Edwards couldn't agree more.

LIVING IN BETWEEN

Yet now I am living with work to be done.

JAMES MONTGOMERY BOICE

PAUL ONCE SAID he desired to depart this life and to be with Christ (Phil. 1:23). That, he thought, would be great gain, would be "far better." I suspect many Christians share Paul's desire. This life and this world have little to interest them. Their hearts are elsewhere. Others may not be so inclined; this world offers them a great deal, and because they are tantalized by it, heaven recedes into the distance.

Both perspectives miss something. Paul did say that he would rather depart, but he also told the Philippians that to live is Christ, adding that "to live in the flesh . . . means fruitful labor for me" (Phil. 1:22). Paul longed to be in heaven, but he also knew that he had to live on earth and that this life can be full of meaning and purpose and value, that this life can be fruitful.

James Montgomery Boice, famous not only for what he said but also for his inimitable voice, received the bleakest news that anyone can receive in April 2000. He was diagnosed with liver cancer. In a matter of months it would take his life. In 1999, just before the diagnosis and after he had written many books and commentaries, he tried his hand at a new genre—hymn-writing. In what would come to be the final year of his life, he authored a dozen hymn texts, and his church's musician and organist, Paul Jones, composed the tunes.

The hymns reflect the doctrines that were close to his heart. One in particular celebrates the great Reformation doctrine that our salvation is by the grace of God alone (Latin: *sola gratia*). In effect, the hymn becomes the story of every Christian's life. We begin as sinners, corrupt and dead. "But God"—a quite profound pair of words—in his compassion and love extends his grace that brings us to new life in Christ (Eph. 2:4-5). Boice then declares in the fourth stanza, "I'll boast in my Savior, all merit decline, and glorify God 'til I die." I venture to guess that if we were writing this hymn, we would more than likely affix a hearty amen and a final period and end it there.

But not Boice. He pushes on, adding a fifth stanza that begins, "Yet now I am living with work to be done." His own life is a testament to his determination to live in between. Even as cancer robbed him of his energy, he persevered, writing hymns and serving God in his final days. Boice reveled in the glory of the age to come, and in the meantime his eternal home had everything to do with his life on earth. *Now*, he tells us, we have work to do.

If there was anyone who longed for heaven, it would be Dietrich Bonhoeffer. Imprisoned by the Nazis, Bonhoeffer spent the last years of his life in his 6 x 9 cell. At first he despaired and almost succumbed to the temptation of taking his own life.

Then he found, by grace, an entirely new perspective on life in between. From his cell at Tegel Prison he wrote, "The Christian hope of resurrection . . . sends a man back to his life on earth in a wholly new way." "The Christian," he continued, "has no last line of escape available from earthly tasks and difficulties." Then he concluded, "This world must not be prematurely written off."[1] Within the year he would be hanged at Flossenbürg Concentration Camp. Also within that year Dietrich Bonhoeffer wrote some of his most lasting and challenging work. Both Bonhoeffer and Boice were determined to live in between and not write off life in this world.

A THIRD WAY

Not everyone shares Boice's and Bonhoeffer's perspective. As mentioned earlier, some are overly consumed with the life to come. They are, in the words of the old adage, so heavenly-minded that they are of no earthly good. They're like Thales, credited as the first philosopher among the Greeks. The stars and galaxies intrigued Thales. He thought that somehow the answer to the ultimate question of the meaning of life was above. So devoted was he to this task that he would often walk peering into the skies, entirely oblivious to his surroundings. Legend has it that on one occasion, as he was deeply absorbed in looking up at the stars and paying no attention to the ground beneath, he took a terrible tumble. Some are so heavenly-minded that, like Thales, they're dangerous to themselves and others.

In the end, such a view is little more than escapism. Those who adopt it tend to care very little for life this side of glory, often think of people as mere "souls," and many times find themselves unsure of how to go about living. In the Middle Ages, folks of this persuasion entered a monastery and, cloistered within its walls, served God on a spiritual plane. In the modern world, such people tend to live in monasteries of their own making, safe within the shelter of its walls. These monasteries take different forms for different people.

Some suffer from what we might call a heightened eschatology, the word theologians use to describe biblical teaching about the end times. Millard Erickson refers to those who obsess over these doctrines as "eschatamaniacs." All these folks talk about is the Rapture or the Second Coming of Christ, and they certainly know their book of Revelation. There is nothing wrong with longing for Christ to come back. Paul and Peter and even John did just that, and they all in various ways command us to do the same. But they also remind us that our upward vision and longing should not distract us from the path that is before us on earth.

Peter tells the recipients of his second letter that this world will burn (3:10). But he also tells them that while we live on this earth, we are to live a life of holiness and grow in grace (vv. 11-18). Paul tells us that "the day of the Lord" is coming. He also informs us, however, that we are to spend the intervening days encouraging one another and working, not idly passing the time (1 Thess. 5:1-11). At one point he even commands us that whenever we have the opportunity, we are to do good to everyone—a command that clearly entails making a difference in *this* world (Gal. 6:10). The problem with an overzealous eschatology is that it distracts us from our calling and task in this world, just like those who entered a monastery.

Others construct a modern monastery by adopting a

"fortress mentality." They refuse to live in this world and instead construct an entirely Christian one, from which they rarely break out. They are consumed by Christian radio stations and Christian bookstores, and when they need their faucets fixed, they make sure that it's done by a Christian plumber. If they can't be in heaven, they'll simply construct one on earth. They wholeheartedly agree with Paul that to die is gain. They're just not sure how to say along with Paul that life "in the flesh" (that is, in the body, on earth) is "fruitful labor" (Phil. 1:22).

On the other hand, in contrast to monastery Christians, whether literally or figuratively, some are distracted by this world and risk being consumed by it. For them, the Christian faith means little more than learning how to be a better parent or how to balance a checkbook or manage a business or find inner serenity. To them, this world eclipses the next. They wouldn't come within a hundred yards of a monastery. They are consumed by this world's agenda and are driven by its passions. They may very well use Christian lingo to baptize their pursuits, but their hearts are not directed toward their home. To put a twist on the old adage, these folks are so earthly-minded that heaven doesn't look very attractive to them. As for life on this earth, they would feel quite claustrophobic within monastery walls. They would much prefer to break out and blend in, perhaps even to be trendsetters. Rather than withdraw from the world, they're right at home in it. Paul's belief that "to die is gain" doesn't make much sense to them.

The answer to the dilemma lies deeper than simply seeking a balance between being earthly- and heavenly-minded. The answer only comes as we adopt a radically different perspective, the perspective that Boice declares in his hymn, that Bonhoeffer proclaims from his prison cell, that Paul captures in his letter to the Philippians, and that Edwards preaches in his sermons. This radical perspective saves us from escapism on the one hand and from a life that is distracted and absorbed and consumed by this world on the other. In between being too heavenly-minded or too earthly-minded there is a third way: living in this world from the perspective of the next. To state the matter more directly, it's a vision of heaven on earth.

What Paul, Boice, and Bonhoeffer put so well others have also observed. No miraculous transporter takes John Bunyan's character Christian straight to heaven once he comes to the cross and the burden of sin rolls off his back. Quite the opposite. *Pilgrim's Progress* recalls sometimes painful and sometimes triumphant steps as Christian makes his way from the cross to the Celestial City, his eternal home. He faces challenges such as the Giant of Despair in Doubting Castle or the taunting voices of the masses drunk on consumerism in Vanity Fair. As Christian makes his way, sometimes quite slowly, his journey eases as he learns to live in light of the realities of the Celestial City. He longs to enter its gates, to be at home, but he must go through the journey. His eyes are on both the City ahead and the road beneath his feet. To Bunyan's fictional character we might add Bunyan himself, who in his imprisonment and in his ministry modeled living in between, living the vision of heaven on earth. But perhaps no single figure captures this idea more poignantly than Jonathan Edwards (1703-1758).

Most of us—if we have read anything by Edwards—have read his famous sermon "Sinners in the Hands of an Angry God." We know that Edwards has a great deal to say about hell.

What we may not know is that Edwards has a far greater amount to say about heaven.

A (VERY) BRIEF LIFE OF JONATHAN EDWARDS

Jonathan Edwards was born, as the saying has it, in interesting times. The old Puritan world was unraveling, and a new world was emerging. The Colonies were on the cusp of becoming a new nation as Edwards's life came to an end. Jonathan Edwards, however, had both feet firmly planted in the Puritan world, and he was a citizen of the British Empire (he always made reference to "our nation" in his correspondence with his Scottish friends). Yet, being in the Colonies did have its effect upon him.

His father was a minister, as were his grandfathers and uncles and cousins and sons. As the only son to Timothy and Sarah Stoddard Edwards, he had ten sisters (that alone should secure him a place in history). His sisters taught him Latin, especially when his father was away serving as chaplain for various British regiments in skirmishes with the Canadians and Indians. His mother instilled in him a love for books and learning and the life of the mind. His father modeled for him in plain view the trials and triumphs of the ministry. After his Harvard education, his father settled in the town of East Windsor, Connecticut, along the lush and picturesque Connecticut River Valley. He was minister in that town for sixty years.

East Windsor was, for the Reverend Timothy Edwards, the best and the worst of times. The earliest surviving letter from Jonathan is to his sister Mary, living in Boston at the time, in which he tells of "a remarkable stirring and outpouring of the

Spirit of God." A revival had come to East Windsor. We have a letter from Timothy Edwards to his deacons a decade earlier. He thanks them for receipt of his salary in 1705, reminding them that his salary from 1704 was still outstanding, not to mention his salary from 1703. And through all of the good and trying times, young Jonathan learned.

By the age of thirteen he was ready for college and went off to Yale. He received his Bachelor's degree (1720) and Master's degree (1723). In between, as a nineteen-year-old, he pastored his first church. A splinter group from a church split, the church happened to be located around the vicinity of modern-day Wall Street and Broad Street in New York City. Edwards meticulously prepared his sermons, rode horseback along the Hudson River, and managed somehow to counsel the splinter group to reunite. Putting himself out of a job, Edwards traveled home to write his Master's thesis. He then stayed on at Yale as a tutor or instructor for two years. At New Haven he noticed—or perhaps more accurately, was absolutely stricken by—Sarah Pierpont.

Eventually he was called to serve as assistant minister to his maternal grandfather, Solomon Stoddard, at Northampton, Massachusetts, directly north of his childhood home and along his beloved Connecticut River. He arrived in 1727, and in that same year he married Sarah. Like his own family, they too would have eleven children, with three boys and eight girls. Shortly after they were married, Stoddard died, leaving Edwards as sole pastor of one of the largest churches in the Colonies.

In the 1730s revival came to Northampton and to the other towns along the Connecticut River. In the first years of the

1740s, another wave of revival swept through the same region, only this time it went far beyond as it encompassed the entire Colonies. Known as the "Great Awakening," this event was second only to the Revolutionary War in its impact. Edwards, along with fellow revivalist from England George Whitefield, was right at the center of it.

But, as he had learned as a boy, trials follow triumphs. In the middle to late 1740s, Jonathan Edwards came down off the mountain and walked through the valley. This particular valley was a conflict with his church that would eventually lead to his ouster. Edwards had noticed that after the revivals his formerly spiritually warm congregation turned cold. In response, among other things, he ended a practice instituted by his grandfather and one with which he had long felt uncomfortable, that of an open Communion table. Stoddard held Communion to be a "converting ordinance" and opened admission to all, whether or not they professed faith in Christ. When Edwards put an end to Stoddard's practice, that did not set well with the staid powers of the congregation. In good congregational fashion, they voted Edwards out on June 22, 1750.

Edwards headed to the frontier. In order to do this in 1750, he only had to travel about fifty miles west to the recently established outpost town of Stockbridge, Massachusetts, home to 250 or so Mohawks and Mohicans and a dozen English families. Edwards, revivalist, scholar, and pastor, now became a missionary. For seven years he served, and here too he had his ups and downs. He was then invited, in the winter months of 1757, to become president of Princeton University. He accepted, arriving there in January 1758. After just a few weeks in office, he received a smallpox inoculation, in part because he wanted to show the students they had nothing to fear and in part due to his lifelong fascination with advancements in the sciences. He, however, contracted "a secondary fever," in the words of the attending physician. After a short but intense illness, Edwards died on March 22, 1758. But not before he left a legacy that continues to impact the church.

Writings from the scholarly world on Edwards surpass that of his fellow colonials Benjamin Franklin and George Washington. Theologians, pastors, and laity alike continue to turn to his thought and life. Now, three centuries after his birth, he continues to have something to say. We'll return to these biographical episodes in the ensuing chapters. This sketch merely serves to give us the big picture of his life, against which we can see his ideas, not the least of which is his vision for living in between, his vision for life in this world as we make our pilgrimage to the next.[2]

CAPTURING EDWARDS'S VISION

This vision for living in between shines brightly through his life and sermons. He traced it through Scripture, meditated upon it in quiet moments, and wrestled with its implications. He then stood in the pulpit and heralded it in all of its simplicity and beauty to his congregations at Northampton and Stockbridge. In his hands, this perspective became a most compelling message precisely because it so transformed his own life. With a clear-eyed view of what it means to live in between, he had a vision of the Christian life that brought the realities and nature of the life to come to bear upon this present age. His vision of the church consisted of a redeemed community living in this life according to the principles and dictates of the life to come. He was consumed by heaven. But this was no mere ethereal vision. He did not fall prey to the escapism that plagues so many earnest Christians. His vision of the next life had everything to do with this life. For Jonathan Edwards, living in between meant living the vision of heaven on earth. This is the truly good life, the only life worth living.

But, of course, all was not well in Northampton and in Stockbridge. This vision in his preaching did not always get worked out in practice. The redeemed community did not always live in light of heaven, and even Edwards himself sometimes upset the balance and lost the sharp edge of his heavenly vision. He was, after all, not a superhero. These shortcomings, however, do not detract from the power of his example. In fact, they may serve to make it even more compelling.

A few years back an advertisement for a national chain of fitness centers ended by saying that if having a fit and athletic body came in a bottle, everyone would have one. I often wondered about the effectiveness of that campaign. In effect, the ad tells us that there are no shortcuts to fitness—you don't just snap your fingers. We know that's true, but we don't like to be told this; we prefer an easier way. If Edwards could have waved a wand over his congregation, or over his own life for that matter, and could have made them and himself immune to being consumed by this world or safe from the escapist tendencies of heavenly-minded Christians, he would have certainly done so without hesitation. There is no wand to wave, however. The ad is right; it doesn't come in a bottle.

Edwards did live out the vision, but not always perfectly. We can learn from him both when he got it right and when he missed the mark. In the remaining chapters, we will listen in on some of his sermons as we try to understand the art of living in between, of living the vision of heaven on earth.

Each of the following chapters takes its cue from a particular sermon of Edwards. In the second chapter, his final sermon from a series on 1 Corinthians 13, titled "Heaven Is a World of Love," sets the stage for us as we make our way to heaven. Chapter Three looks at "The Pleasantness of Religion," a little-known sermon from his early years. This offers us a different perspective on living as citizens of heaven than we typically tend to have. Here we see Edwards telling us that Christianity is the pursuit of pleasure in this life—not something we often attribute to a Puritan. In Chapter Four, Edwards points us to our call to live and act justly in his sermon "Much in Deeds of Charity." Here we'll also see how Edwards modeled his teaching as he lived and worked among the Mohicans and Mohawks at Stockbridge. Sometimes we look at the world around us and resign ourselves to the idea that justice will only come in the next world. While that's true, it does not excuse doing nothing in the meantime. Edwards helps us think about how we can be subversive agents in an unjust world.

None of us likes to wait. We didn't like to wait when we were kids, and we haven't grown out of it yet. Edwards's sermon "I Know My Redeemer Lives" offers an intriguing perspective on what to do while we wait, the subject of Chapter Five. Chapter Six adds the sermon "Serving God in Heaven" to the mix, as Edwards insightfully challenges us to see that what we will do in heaven is a pretty good model for what to do now. Writing to his daughter, he once shared his desire that all of his family "meet there at last," his goal that they all meet in heaven. This goal was not simply to be met at the end of life's journey.

For Edwards, it informed him and directed him every step of the way as he lived in between this life and the life to come. We'll look at this dynamic perspective in the final chapter as we peer into his sermon "The True Christian's Life a Journey Toward Heaven."

Edwards's vision for living in between was not simply a vision for him. It was also not original with him. It is woven into the very fabric of the Bible. As we listen to Edwards, we'll hear the echoes of this glorious theme from Scripture. We'll come to see that we are pilgrims, bound for another world and called to live according to foreign customs. But we'll also learn that the journey matters. We'll learn the value of living in between.

2

ON THE WAY
TO HEAVEN

*If heaven is a world of love,
then the way to heaven is the way of love.*

JONATHAN EDWARDS, 1738

ON THE SURFACE, Edwards seems an unlikely spokesperson for living the vision of heaven on earth. He seems to fall more on the side of being too heavenly-minded. We tend to think of him as the consummate Puritan, so enthralled with the life to come that this life and its pleasures had very little hold on him. His eyes were only directed up, certainly not down. The only thing worthwhile in this life, goes the caricature of Edwards, is to escape it, and to escape the wrath of God that is to come. This, however, only *appears* to be the case. Dig a little deeper, and you will find that his vision of heaven has everything to do with life on earth. He had a great deal to say about heaven, but it wasn't simply relegated to the sweet by-and-by. He had a great deal to say about this life that far outstrips merely escaping it and the wrath to come. This is no more the case than in his sermon "Heaven Is a World of Love," our focus in this chapter (an abridgment of this sermon appears in the Appendix of this book).

WILL THE REAL JONATHAN EDWARDS PLEASE STAND UP?

In 1738 Edwards began a sermon series on Paul's famous poem in 1 Corinthians 13. Edwards called the series "Charity and Its Fruits," using the King James Version's word for love. His series reached a crescendo with the final sermon, "Heaven Is a World of Love."[1]

This is not the Edwards that most people know. The over-whelming judgment of contemporary readers is that Edwards was dour and calloused and that when he preached, he breathed the smoke of hellfire and brimstone harangues. This stems from the one sermon of his that most are familiar with, "Sinners in the Hands of an Angry God." In this sermon Edwards piles up the imagery to display the terrors and horrors awaiting a sinful humanity and in the process offers the perfect foil for those who dislike both the God of wrath and judgment and those who preach him. In fact, a popular image of Edwards is a woodcut from the twentieth century that has Edwards looking grim and emaciated as he holds up his hand as if to bar the way to God and stop us dead in our tracks. This image of Edwards could not be more wrong, and this judgment of him could not be more ironic.

It is ironic because his sermons overflow with the words *sweetness*, *pleasure*, *joy*, *love*, and *beauty*. Edwards never pulled back from proclaiming the wrath of God on sin, but he just as forcefully and readily proclaimed the abundant mercy and grace of a good and loving God. And this language meets us on every page of the "Charity and Its Fruits" sermons. By the time he gets to the final installment, it's as if the floodgates are opened and he can no longer contain the overflow of God's goodness, pleasure, sweetness, beauty, and love. If you want a one-sided picture of Edwards, simply be content with reading "Sinners in the Hands of an Angry God." If you want the full picture, read it and then read "Heaven Is a World of Love."

In "Heaven Is a World of Love," Edwards invites us to imagine a world. It is not, however, an imaginary world. It's the real world of the life to come. In this world, love dominates. The mutual love of God the Father and Jesus Christ the Son and the Holy Spirit fills heaven. Edwards's portrait of heaven has at its center God, an infinite fountain of love. There in heaven he dwells in full Trinitarian splendor. Love doesn't simply trickle along in streams but flows forth in rivers. Eventually, Edwards tells us, "these rivers swell, as it were, to an ocean of love, in which the souls of the ransomed may bathe in the sweetest enjoyment, and their hearts, as it were, be deluged with love." There is a perfect union within the Godhead that flows out to God's people.

LOVE SUPREME

In heaven, love and union reign supreme without obstacles and hindrances. There are no petty jealousies or the posturing of individuals advancing their own selfish agendas. We will love God for his own sake, not for what we might gain. The saints will love each other without even a hint of selfishness or ulterior motives. As Edwards puts it, "There shall be nothing within themselves to clog or hinder the saints in heaven in the exercises and expressions of love." In heaven, love will be perfect and pure and holy. In heaven, love will not go unrequited. There will be no disappointment, no shattered hopes, and no unfulfilled desires. Love and union reign supreme in Edwards's vision of the life to come. Shakespeare has Hamlet say, "Suit the action to the word, the word to the action." When it comes to life in heaven, love is the suitable word.

In the meat of the sermon, the doctrine portion, Edwards explores God as the fountain and source of love in heaven, his creatures as the heavenly objects of love, and the "excellent circumstances" of heaven that result in the "happy effects and fruits" of this pure and divine love—all of which make heaven a perfect world. So Edwards concludes this portion of the sermon with one copious sentence:

> And thus the saints will love and reign in love, and in that godlike joy that is its blessed fruit, such as eye hath not seen, nor ear heard, nor hath ever entered into the heart of man in this world to conceive; and thus in the full sunlight of the throne, enraptured with joys that are for ever increasing, and yet for ever full, they shall live and reign with Christ and God for ever and ever.

So far in the sermon he has cast a grand vision of heaven, exhausting language to display its glorious radiance. But Edwards does not stop here. He has yet to make his application. He doesn't simply point his congregation to heaven; he doesn't simply fill his congregation with blissful thoughts of glory. He points them to heaven with one hand, while with the other he directs their attention back to earth. He wants these blissful and high and lofty thoughts to land squarely on earth. In another's hands, this sermon would be gushy and sentimental, even trite.

Edwards has a way, however, of making it true and honest and concrete.

In one of his points of application, Edwards offers us some advice as we wait for heaven and the fulfillment of God's promises to us. His vision of heaven helps ease that tension of waiting by reminding us of the taste of the happiness and love that we enjoy now. This mere taste of God's goodness, he argues, is not only enough to satisfy us while we wait, it also whets our appetite for more to come. We are convinced by our own experience, Edwards tells us, that not only is God good, but he is the best good. While we have had only a taste of his goodness and the happiness to come, "such happiness suits [our] disposition and appetite and wishes above all other things; and not only above all things that we have but above all that we can conceive it possible that we could have. The world does not afford anything like it." This isn't simply waiting for God's goodness in the future—it's experiencing it now.

As he moves along in the application, however, Edwards is concerned that we do more than passively wait, enjoying happiness. He calls us to action. In the sermon so far, he has handily argued that heaven is a world of love. Now that he's made his case, he draws the logical conclusion. "As heaven is a world of love," he declares, "so the way to heaven is the way of love." He even puts it more boldly: "If you would be in the way to the world of love, you must live a life of love."

For some people, entering heaven will be quite uncomfortable; they won't feel at all at home. The language and the customs will confound them, and they will feel like a stranger in a strange land. These are the folks who, as we saw in the Introduction, are simply too earthly-minded. Of course, I'm overstating the matter. We could certainly wonder if anyone who truly feels this way does indeed love Christ. But there are those who do love Christ who are far too attached to this world. Edwards holds out an opposite standard. For Edwards the model is Enoch, the Old Testament saint whose walk with God was so real and so marked his life that his transition from this world to the next was as natural as simply taking another step (Gen. 5:24; Heb. 11:5). Entering heaven, Edwards argues, should not be startling. Entering heaven should be as natural and comfortable and desirable as returning home after a long trip.

Such smooth transitions as Enoch's, and as that which Edwards holds out for his congregation and for us, only happen when we live in light of heaven, when we agree with Edwards that the way to heaven is no mystery, that the way to heaven corresponds to the very nature of heaven itself. But while we may strive to live in the way of love, and while we long deeply for heaven on earth, we still must contend with earth. We want to love free of hindrances, unclogged, as Edwards might say, but we have hindrances and obstacles and clogs in our way.

SPIRITUALITY FOR HUMANS

Perhaps we can gain something from the life of Edwards and some of the struggles that he faced. Edwards, easily the most famous pastor ever born on American soil, was kicked out of his church at Northampton. We could put what Edwards learned from his own experience this way: while "heaven is a world of love," congregations can be full of strife. It may seem that Edwards was the culprit, with too much fire and brimstone preaching, too much berating his congregation. That just wasn't the case, but we'll say more on this later. For now, we need to see that the realities of his ministry with all of its rumblings and strife kept his vision of the redeemed community living the way of love from being fully realized. The realities of life broke in. His heart soared heavenward, while his feet were thrust deep into the ground.

This is not to say that he was conflicted, hopelessly naive, or fatally pessimistic. It is to say that he lived in between. And so do we. We long for heaven. We want peace and love and harmony to rule in our relationships. We want never to be at odds with others, and we don't like conflict. As a two-year-old, my son has the remarkable ability to be honest. He might occasionally be doing something bad, all the while saying through clenched teeth, "Obey, obey, obey." We are just like he is. As Paul put it, we do what we don't want to and don't do that which we know we should (Rom. 7:15). In the words of the Synod of Dort, a council of the church that met in the Netherlands in 1618-19, spots adhere even to our finest garments. Try as hard as we might, living the way of love does not come easily, and more often than not, it comes kicking and screaming. We sin. As Luther said, we sometimes even sin boldly.

Edwards is right: the way to heaven should be the way of love, and that love and harmony should mark us through and through. But this doesn't always happen. Petty jealousies and posturing will dissolve in the sweet by-and-by, but for now they are all too real. We long to say a kind word in a tense situation, take the high road in times of conflict, or go out of our way to serve others before serving our own needs. In reality, our words all too often fuel the fire, and our selfishness crowds out our impulse to lift a hand to help our neighbor.

So how are we to take Edwards's beatific vision? One way

would be to leave it in the future. Such sermons as "Heaven Is a World of Love" may stir us up, may instill within us a longing for our future home. But in the real world, such a vision simply doesn't work. Even if we were capable of living the life of love, we would get trampled on earth. Indeed, this way leaves the application of the sermon where it best belongs, in the future tense. This way reserves optimism for the future only, while pessimism rules the present.

Another way to respond to Edwards's sermon and his beatific vision goes in the opposite direction. This may be best described as naïveté. Here one says rather uncritically that as it is in heaven, so shall it be on earth. The only problem with this view is, in the recent words of Rodney Clapp from his new book *Tortured Wonders*, this is a spirituality for angels, not for human beings. We can't ignore the fact that we are sinners and that those around us are sinners too. If we do the math, we will unfortunately find that sin is exponentially present in this world. And all that sin can have a spoiling effect.

There is a third way. Even those who aren't particularly fond of baseball or those who are diehard fans of another team should admire the doggedly loyal fans of the Boston Red Sox. These fans waited and waited and waited eighty-six years for the title to return to Fenway Park. Stories abound of fans literally longing to stay alive so they could savor victory before they died. One fan bought dozens of shirts commemorating the 2004 World Series victory and placed them on the graves of relatives and friends who were not there to see their beloved Sox triumph. The very next year a similar thing happened to the other Sox, the Chicago White Sox. They hadn't won a World Series since 1917. But 2005 was to be their year.

These fans, both of the Red and White Sox, intently monitored preseason trades, set high hopes for each season to come, and faithfully purchased season tickets. They even, in the best of baseball's folklore traditions, did all they could to break the alleged curses plaguing their teams. Even in the seasons when a World Series bid was nowhere near even a pipe dream, they held out hope that this just might be the year. These fans were the image of grit and determination.

There's a parable here, but the stakes are so much higher than the outcome of the World Series. We too fly in the face of present reality. We bear the marks of our team, and we sound its cheers. Against the odds, we strive to live the way of love on the way to heaven. We never give up hope, and we never waiver in our loyalty. Here is how we begin to live the vision of Jonathan Edwards. We don't throw that vision into the future, nor do we ignore the realities of the present. Living in between means we take both worlds into account. We are on the way to heaven, but we are not there yet. We applaud its breakthroughs in this world, but we know there are far better things to come.

FORETASTES OF THINGS TO COME

Edwards was fully aware that his sermon and its application would be quite challenging. He acknowledges the difficulties of living the vision of heaven on earth, and even accounts for them. First, he tells us that we are to strive to live the way of love. This tells us that it does not come automatically, easily, and certainly not perfectly. But we are nevertheless to strive.

He then says something that, while brief, goes a long way to inspire us to live this unique vision. He tells us that as we strive to live in the way of heaven, we "have, on earth, the foretastes of heavenly pleasures and delights." When we live the way of love, then we have heaven on earth, even if it is in miniature.

John Milton penned a most poignant description of all that was possessed and all that was lost in the Garden of Eden. His *Paradise Lost* portrays a world in the garden not unlike that of the world of heaven that Edwards describes. It is perfect and harmonious and peaceful. Adam and Eve love truly and perfectly, and in the cool of the evening they commune with God himself, unhampered by sin. But with the fall, all is lost. Adam and Eve and the creation and all humanity to follow are plunged into misery. Once Eve succumbs to the serpent and Adam follows suit, the harmony disintegrates, and strife reigns. The relationship of Adam and Eve sours, and a relentless friction overtakes them. As Milton captures it, "Thus they in mutual accusations spent the fruitless hours . . . and of their vain contest appeared no end." When God appears, Adam and Eve can no longer commune with him unhindered. Sin now violates all relationships.

Cornelius Plantinga, Jr. more recently captured the great loss of the fall in the title of his book *Not the Way It's Supposed to Be.*[2] This world was intended to be a world of peace and harmony, a world of *shalom*. And it was such a world in those early days after creation. But sin violated and scandalized and perverted that *shalom*, leaving a world of strife and conflict. Adam and Eve turned on each other and were turned away from God. The ground became cursed. Eventually brother would turn against brother as Cain slew Abel. Like the tragedies befalling the characters in John Steinbeck's modern paraphrase of Genesis in his novel *East of Eden*, strife rips through our relationships, leaving carnage in its wake.

What Milton and Plantinga and Steinbeck all write about we know to be true in our own experience. How easy it is for us to speak an unkind word, how quick we are to judge or misjudge, and how slow we are to ask for and to offer forgiveness. We look at Cain, and with all the smugness we can muster we assure ourselves of how good we are. We shake our heads at the various characters in the Parable of the Good Samaritan as they pass by the beaten and broken traveler left for dead on the side of the road. Yet we commit atrocities against our fellow human beings daily. Of course, we're not murderers, and we would likely not pass by someone in such dire straits. But in small and subtle ways we add to the strife and conflict.

Yet there is hope. As Milton proceeds in his depiction of the fall, he has Adam and Eve make the best of the new normality of their lives. Once they are expelled from the garden, living under the full force of the curse but nevertheless longing for the seed to come to undo their deed of disobedience, Adam and Eve face life with renewed commitment to each other. And so Milton places these loving words in Adam's mouth:

> But rise, let us no more contend, nor blame
> Each other, blamed enough elsewhere, but strive
> In offices of love how we may lighten
> Each other's burden in our share of woe.[3]

Love reigns when we sow harmony where there is strife, when we speak a kind and gracious word into the midst of conflict, when we bring beauty into a world of malice and darkness. Love reigns when we, even in our frailty, offer to ease each other's burdens as we help one another carry our collective share of woe (Gal. 6:2). Milton has Adam make a conscious choice not to do that which now came naturally for him. He has Adam choose love over contention. It is "not the way it's supposed to be," but we can speak to the way that it should be, the way it can be. Redemption and grace provide an answer to our fallen condition that applies not merely to setting things right in the next world—redemption and grace mean we can live differently in this one.

We have heard stories of heroic sacrifice made in the face of intense circumstances—stories of those like Oskar Schindler, who literally brought life and peace to so many Jews trapped in the death grip of the Nazi regime. Or there's the story of the lesser known Raoul Wallenberg, the Swedish-born architect and businessman. Wallenberg found himself in Hungary during the war. Armed with courage and conviction alone, he stood against Hitler's "final solution" to the Jewish problem, leading thousands of Jews to safety and security.[4]

The reality is that few of us will be in such a place and time, and few of us will be called on for such heroic feats. We do, however, have occasion after occasion to make simple contributions to the lives of others. These range from simply passing along a kind word of gratitude to the clerk in the store to committing a few hours to an after-school program for underprivileged children. Virtue comes in all sizes.

We make the contribution when we share the gospel in word and in deed. As we live not just in light of the fall and the realities of a sin-cursed world but also in light of redemption and the promised world to come, we ever so slightly see love reign on this earth.

Edwards tells us that such living based on such choices enabled by God's grace is a foretaste of the life to come. In fact, it is worth hearing how he elaborates this thought. By living the way of love in this world, he tells us that we begin to reflect the image of saints in heaven, we begin to sense the sweet and holy peace that reigns there. He continues:

> Thus, also you may have a sense of the glory of heavenly things, as of God, and Christ, and holiness; and your heart be disposed and opened by holy love to God, and by the spirit of peace and love to men, to a sense of the excellence and sweetness of all that is to be found in heaven. Thus shall the windows of heaven be as it were opened, so that its glorious light shall shine in upon your soul. Thus you may have the evidence of your fitness for that blessed world, and that you arc actually on the way to its possession. And being thus made fit, through grace, for the inheritance of the saints in light, when a few more days shall have passed away, you shall be with them in their blessedness for ever. Happy, three times happy those, who shall thus be found faithful to the end, and then shall be welcomed to the joy of their Lord.

THE GOOD AND THE BAD

This, again, was no mere beatific and ethereal vision. I mentioned earlier that Edwards was voted out of his church. That occurred in 1750. In 1738, when he preached his sermon series on 1 Corinthians 13, that battle was a long way off. But when the strife came, Edwards did not lose sight of the truth and force of his vision of the redeemed community modeling the life of love. In fact, it buoyed him through the rough waters. He was not blameless in the conflict, even though he was on the right side of the issues.

One of the things that Edwards failed to do was to cultivate relationships with his people. Edwards rarely opened up, and when he did, it tended to be in his correspondence with his colleagues in ministry around New England and in Scotland. When he was beginning in ministry at Northampton, he made a choice not to make regular pastoral calls on his parishioners, only seeing them at times when they were, in Puritan language, "soul anxious." Edwards's disposition may have had something to do with that. He was likely more at home with books than with people. Yet, these moves proved fatal when the time of conflict came with his congregation. He simply did not have the support of a congregation behind him. It's hard to point out a single incident where Edwards spoke a harsh word, where he may have lashed out, excepting of course his legitimate challenges from the pulpit. But it's equally hard to find the times when he cultivated relationships with his people.

Such was not the case in his home. His was a busy home. Eleven children were born to Sarah and Jonathan Edwards. Frequent guests stayed in the home, and young ministerial students lived under the Edwards roof as they trained for the ministry. Amidst all of this busyness, love and kindness were not pushed aside. All accounts concur: this was a home where love reigned. The Edwardses dealt with sicknesses and stretched budgets, times of political and national turmoil—these were the days of Indian raids and tense relations with the British and the French. The Edwards family had times of triumph and celebration as well. And in all of it, the "uncommon union" of Jonathan and Sarah that overflowed the home spoke to his commitment to follow the way of love, to lighten his family's burden of woe. Like Milton's Adam, Edwards once challenged husbands to do all they could to seek the good and comfort and happiness of their wives.

So we see in Edwards a mixture. Sometimes he got it right, while at other times he fell short. We see that it is not always easy to live as we are called. We see that while we are on earth, we may long for heaven, we may long for those eternal and future realities to be just as real and true here and now, but we realize that won't always be the case. The reality is that we are fallen human beings living in a fallen world. It would be wrong, however, to conclude that because we are sinners in a fallen world, Edwards's sermon "Heaven Is a World of Love" doesn't work. It would even be wrong to see this sermon and its goals as a nice piece of inspiration but short on real-world application. This is not the brass ring on the merry-go-round. It's our calling. The life of love is not on reserve until the future; it is to be lived now in this world.

And in this world we are called to live as Christians. We are ambassadors of another land, with a different set of customs and laws, and even a different language. As we represent this land and its Monarch, we must bear the marks of our home. We must live by its customs and speak its language, however foreign they may be.

Jonathan Edwards was right. If heaven is a world of love, then the way to heaven is the way of love. Easier said than done, to be sure, but as we live the way of love, we find that God's grace meets us at every turn. And we "have, on earth, the foretaste of heavenly pleasures and delights."

3

BEING GOOD CITIZENS

Plant sequoias.

WENDELL BERRY

ACCORDING TO PAUL in Philippians 3:20, everything I've written so far is wrong. "Our citizenship is in heaven." Paul wants us to have both feet firmly planted there. In fact, Paul's admonition that we are citizens of heaven comes on the heels of his rebuke of those governed by earthly pursuits and physical appetites, those whose god, as he colorfully puts it, is their belly (v. 19). We shouldn't live with one foot in this world and one foot in the next, as I have been suggesting. Instead, both feet must be firmly planted in heaven. We are, after all, aliens and strangers, pilgrims on a journey from this world to the next.

To add fuel to the fire of the rebuke, we could couple Paul's admonition to be heavenly citizens with Peter's rather urgent reminder in 2 Peter 3:10-12 that this world and all of the work in it, not to mention the heavens, will someday burn, dissolve, and be no more. We, especially North American Christians, should be a little less fond of our citizenship in this world.

I have no doubt that this is true. Yet, there seems to be something wrong. Something wrong, that is, not so much with the idea of Paul and Peter, but perhaps with the application of these texts. The old saying goes something like this: *Why polish the brass on a sinking ship?* In other words, this world will burn someday, so we shouldn't get too caught up in it. The only problem with the mind-set this saying embodies is that we are still here, and so is this world. Even if it is a bit of a sinking ship, it's still the world God made, and it's still the world in which God has called us to live. We are citizens of heaven, but we're not there yet. We are on a pilgrim journey to the world to come. But for now we're living in this world. Perhaps we need to revolutionize our thinking both about this world and about our citizenship.

BRINGING ROME TO PHILIPPI

Paul's metaphor of citizenship only makes sense in its first-century context. Paul could rely on his citizenship to help him out of a legal bind, for being a Roman citizen meant having great privileges. The citizenship metaphor, however, extends far beyond privileges and rights such as a fair trial. The Roman Empire was a conglomerate, a patchwork quilt of nations and city-states. For the Empire to run smoothly required uniformity. Greek was the official language, the pantheon of gods the official religion, and Caesar and the Roman Senate the law of the land. This uniformity also came about through Rome's program of decreasing national and ethnic identities and increasing their central identity. One's allegiance was not first to Philippi or to

Israel or to Alexandria; it was first to Rome. Rome would deport citizens of the various nations and city-states it conquered, dispersing them throughout the Empire. Rome would also force its citizens from the established cities to move even to the far reaches of the Empire. Long before the waves of immigration made America the great melting pot of the modern world, the Roman Empire attempted to bring the entire Mediterranean world under one roof. One was a Roman first, a Philippian or a Jew or an Alexandrian second.[1]

So, to be a Roman citizen living in Philippi or wherever did not mean that you spent your time pining away for the good life in the city of Rome. It did not mean that you longed to get out of Philippi, out of Asia Minor, and back to where your heart was—the city of Rome. Instead, it meant that you were entrusted with the task of bringing Rome and all of its achievements and glory to Philippi or Jerusalem or Alexandria, wherever you found yourself to be. Gordon Fee, in his scholarly commentary on Philippians, puts this together for us: "Just as Philippi was a colony of Rome, whose citizens thereby exemplified the life of Rome in the province of Macedonia, so the citizens of the 'Heavenly Commonwealth' were to function as a colony of heaven in that outpost of Rome."[2]

For example, in A.D. 596 Augustine of Canterbury, not to be confused with St. Augustine who wrote *The Confessions* and *City of God*, made the remarkable trek from Rome all the way through the Alps of Northern Italy, through France, and across the strait of the Sea of Dover. He settled first at Canterbury and eventually commissioned bishops for London and York. Along with him he brought Roman religion, which by that time was Christianity, and Roman language, which by that time was

47

Latin, and Roman architecture and engineering, in the form of wall-building and viaducts. Augustine of Canterbury was far from home. So he brought his home to where he was. He brought Rome to Britain.

This context sheds light on Paul's use of the citizenship metaphor. Christians do not reveal their heavenly citizenship by simply pining away for the blessed life to come. Rather, they show their citizenship by bringing heaven to earth. Our calling is not to sit along the sidelines and wait for the world to come. Instead, our calling is to bring heaven here, to live in light of heaven's realities now, to show the citizens of these earthly and temporal countries that there is a far better, eternal country. In the words of C. S. Lewis, we are to point out to those who live in the Shadowlands that there is a real world to come. But we are to do more than that. We best point the way to the world to come when we offer glimpses of that world in this one. We point the way to heaven when we speak its language and live by its customs on earth.

Just because this world will burn does not mean that we should leave it rotting on the vine. God put Adam and Eve in the garden to cultivate it. As they did, the garden would reveal the presence and the glory of its Creator at every turn, displayed with the dawn of every new day. Though this world is fallen and sin-cursed, it remains God's world. He desires that we cultivate it, and even that we enjoy it. Even as a nineteen-year-old, Jonathan Edwards understood this to be true.

EDWARDS AND THE PLEASURE ARGUMENT

As a young man, nineteen going on twenty, Jonathan Edwards took his first pastorate. He found himself pastoring a splinter group of a church split, not the most desirable situation. It was a Presbyterian church in New York City—the same congregation remains to this day as New York City's First Presbyterian Church. The church met in the vicinity of Broad and Wall Streets. The splinter group met somewhere down by the docks of what has come to be one of the world's busiest harbors. It was a very small group, and Edwards's pastoral duties at the time largely amounted to preaching sermons—a bad thing for a perfectionist like Edwards. He would write out his sermons seven or eight times, meticulously preparing them. In the process he did something right. In just a few months he was able to counsel the splinter group into reuniting.

One of the sermons that comes from this period of Edwards's pastoral ministry is "The Pleasantness of Religion."[3] It is actually an apologetic or evangelistic sermon, but one that most Christians would benefit from hearing. In it Edwards develops what I have termed the pleasure argument, an argument for Christianity that goes something like this: We should be Christians because of the sheer pleasure that it brings. And Edwards wasn't even talking about the life to come. We should be Christians, the argument goes in full, because of the pleasure it brings *in this life*. It needs to be said that Edwards wasn't talking about a prosperity gospel. More on that later.

Over the centuries, philosophers and theologians have marshaled any number of apologetic arguments for Christianity and for God. Some bear quite sophisticated names. There are the cosmological and teleological arguments, arguments that today tend to be referred to as the argument from intelligent design. These two arguments, with roots in Plato and Aristotle, were developed by such great thinkers as Thomas Aquinas in the

Middle Ages and many profound thinkers and scientists in the modern age. The world exists, the cosmological argument goes (*cosmological* comes from the Greek word *cosmos*, meaning "world"), and since something can't come from nothing, the world must have a source or an origin. The teleological argument (from the Greek word *telos*, which means "purpose" or "design") adds that not only does the world exist, but it is orderly and purposeful. Other theologians and thinkers have spoken of the rather complicated ontological argument. When asked if he believed in God, Mark Twain responded with one word, "Israel," referring to what may be called the historical or providential argument. This argument looks to God's actions in human history as evidence of his existence.

Into this arena of arguments, Jonathan Edwards throws his own: *the argument from pleasure*. Believe in God, believe the claims of Christianity to be true, he tells his congregation huddled by the docks of New York's harbor, for the pleasure of it, for the sweetness of it. Or as he puts it, "It would be worth the while to be religious, if it were only for the pleasantness of it." And Edwards's pleasure argument tells us something about living in between. It tells us that as citizens of heaven, we are to bring heaven, with all of its joys and delights, pleasure and sweetness, to earth. This is a revolutionary way of thinking about our life as pilgrims in this world as we journey on to the next, a revolutionary way of thinking about our heavenly citizenship.

HONEY IS GOOD

Edwards chose Proverbs 24:13-14 as the text for his sermon "The Pleasantness of Religion," which he preached sometime late in the year 1723. It is not a very Puritan sermon. At least not in the way we often caricature the Puritans. H. L. Mencken, America's curmudgeonly newspaperman and wordsmith, put it this way: "A Puritan is anyone who fears that somewhere, someone might just be having a good time." The Puritans were, the caricature goes, dour and sour, preachers of gloom and doom, grim-faced, and even a little mean.

As is often the case, reality disappoints. Because of his sermon "Sinners in the Hands of an Angry God," Edwards typically vies as the poster child for this Puritan caricature. But listen to what he has to say in this sermon: "God has given us of his redundant bounty many things for the delight of our senses, for our pleasure and gratification." Then he adds, "Religion allows us to take the full comfort of our meat and drink, all reasonable pleasures that are to be enjoyed in conversation or recreation; allows the gratification of all our natural appetites. And there are none of the five senses but what we are allowed to please and gratify." Edwards's call to eat, drink, and be merry as we enjoy the good hand of God is poles apart from Mencken's unwarranted condemnation of the Puritans. Honey, Edwards learned from Proverbs, is good. We shouldn't keep ourselves from enjoying it.

Edwards proceeds to offer a number of reasons why religion, by which he means Christianity, is pleasant. First, it helps one realize how to fully enjoy sensory pleasure. "The wicked man," Edwards tells us, "gluts himself" with pleasure, and pleasure boomerangs into pain. Most of us have more than likely experienced the temptation of a smorgasbord. At the time having a little bit of this and a little bit of that, which amounts to a lot all together, seems fun and enjoyable. But afterward reality, in the form of an upset stomach, sets in. Edwards uses this very example, though smorgasbords come a bit after his time. Edwards makes a comparison: "He that at a feast feeds with temperance has much greater pleasure of what he eats and drinks than he that gluts himself and vomits it up again."

The same is true of sexual pleasure. Within God's intentions, within the bounds of marriage, sex is pleasurable and delightful. Outside the bounds of those intentions, that which was intended for pleasure, and may even give momentary and temporary pleasure, eventually turns destructive. Sexual promiscuity has its consequences. Against all of these dead-end and misguided pursuits of pleasure, Edwards notes how the godly, due to their respect for God's intentions, truly and deeply enjoy the pleasures of this life.

Second, the wicked, even while enjoying the pleasures of this life, have "the sting of conscience" to deal with. Our culture has gone to great lengths to overcome the drawback of a convicting conscience. We have developed quite a knack for distraction, for anesthetizing ourselves to our true condition. We bend over backwards to silence the still, small voice of conscience. Our culture may have succeeded in quieting the conscience, but it's not able to silence it. Conscience's sting accompanies the delights and pleasures of this world. But this is not so for the Christian. The Christian partakes of such pleasures, appropriately enjoyed, "peaceably," as Edwards puts it, and not in "slavish fear."

What's more, Christians enjoy the pleasures of this world as tokens of God's love. Edwards observes, "The earthly comforts of the Christian are also very much sweetened by the consideration of the love of God, that God is their Father and friend and gives them these blessings from love to them, and because he delights in them."

Finally, Christianity is pleasant because it affords pleasures far beyond anything temporal or sensory or physical. Edwards lists no fewer than nine things here. Among them is this: "There is a very great delight the Christian enjoys in the sight he has of the glory and excellency of God." We delight in seeing pieces of art, "splendid buildings," and even "beautiful faces." But God is "the most beautiful, the most glorious, the most wonderful Being in the world." This is a heavenly vision or perspective that must orient all that we do and experience in this world. We as Christians know what true delight is because as Christians we have a taste of the goodness of God, we have a glimpse of his beauty. Citizens of heaven possess in miniature the glory to come, which gives us perspective for living as temporary citizens in this world.

The ultimate pleasure the Christian enjoys is God himself. John Piper has found this to be one of the remarkable, if not *the* remarkable, insights of Jonathan Edwards. When we come to Christ, he gives us many wonderful things. What's more, he enables us to enjoy all of them, both spiritual and physical things. But the greatest gift God gives us is himself. He longs for us to enjoy him. This is not a gift for the future only—it's a gift we should enjoy now.[4]

PURSUING PLEASURE

Edwards concludes his sermon with a brief application. It is worthwhile to be a Christian because of the "delight and pleasantness of it . . . hence we may learn that sinners are left without any manner of objection against religion." Non-Christians,

Edwards observes, "commonly fly" to the unpleasantness of Christianity in their reason to reject it. To put it in a contemporary fashion, many contend that becoming a Christian means saying a long, sad good-bye to fun. Edwards actually locates the blame for that thinking squarely on the shoulders of Christians: "The most common argument that is used to urge men to godliness is the pleasures of the life to come." We forget that such pleasures have little impact on many non-Christians, who are in hot "pursuit of the pleasures of this life."

Edwards suggests something radical in response. Why not beat them at their own game? Or as he puts it, "Now we will fight them with their own weapons." Christianity promises reward in the life to come, but it also promises a "reward in this life." And lest we think Edwards is an early version of a prosperity-peddling televangelist, we must bear in mind that for him, the greatest pleasure is found in the glory and excellency of Christ. Edwards recalls the testimony of Paul from 2 Corinthians 6:10: "As sorrowful, yet always rejoicing; as poor, yet making many rich; as having nothing, yet possessing everything."

Paul could calculate all of his experiences with a new math because his heavenly citizenship afforded him a new perspective. When we adopt the new perspective afforded by our heavenly citizenship, this world opens before us in entirely new ways. We come to see the true meaning of pleasure and joy, sweetness and beauty, definitions that only make sense when we live in this world as citizens of heaven. As a nineteen-year-old, this was Edwards's apologetic for Christianity.

Perhaps an illustration will help us see the cogency of Edwards's apologetic. Many Christians—scholars, clergy, and laity alike—have made good arguments against the Mormon Church. They rightly see through its façade and straight to its dangers and deceptions. Many of these same people own a recording of the Mormon Tabernacle Choir or at least stand in awe when they hear the Mormon Tabernacle Choir. Amidst all of its lies, the Mormon Church understands the power of beauty, the power of pleasure. Beauty, and the pleasure it affords, is compelling, and so we buy recordings of the Mormon Tabernacle Choir.

The Mormon Church invests great resources in maintaining the choir and the famous tabernacle with all of its acoustic perfection in which they perform, all for the purpose of drawing us in. I'm not trying to argue that it's a double standard to decry Mormon Church practice and yet enjoy listening to the Mormon Tabernacle Choir. Instead I'm drawing a parallel here, one that we as Christians should learn. Beauty, and the pleasure it affords, is compelling. Coupled with truth, it's downright dangerous.

I'm afraid we have lost the power of beauty, both for us and for our apologetics. We should point to the splash of color that autumn months bring to the trees as a testimony to the goodness of our Creator. We should pause before a masterpiece of art, and we should stand silent before a piece of music artfully composed and perfectly executed. We should, as Edwards reminds us, enjoy the sweet taste of honey.

My wife and I are parents of young children. Just about everyone we talk with tells us to enjoy these years because they go by so quickly. "Love your children," they say. "Before you know it, they'll be all grown up and gone." We're already realizing how fast the months and years seem to slip by. In fact, for all of us our lives in this world—especially when held up to the measure of eternity—are whizzing by. While we are here, we should enjoy the world God has made for us. We should use our talents to make this world a better place. Our lives should contribute to the pleasure of others.

Of course, we need to be careful that in seeking to enjoy this world we do not become too attached to it. But on the other hand, we risk letting it pass by without taking full advantage of enjoying it and enjoying all that comes from the good hand of God (James 1:17). The years do go by quickly.

We also can't ignore the fact that amidst all of the beauty, there abounds much ugliness in our sin-fallen world. The treacherous chambers of the human heart have wreaked havoc over the centuries. Suffering and weakness attend many, drowning out the beauty and the deep joy and pleasure that beauty brings. There is disharmony alongside harmony, ugliness alongside beauty. In such dire circumstances, the tendency is to merely long for this old earth to burn, for our bodies, in the words of Hamlet, to "melt, thaw and resolve [themselves] into a dew." The temptation is to cry out in utter frustration, "How weary, stale, flat and unprofitable seem to me all the uses of this world."[5] At such times we must remember that the God who will someday create the new heavens and the new earth is the same God who created these heavens and this earth. And we are called to be ambassadors of this Creator.

Truth is powerful. When truth is accompanied by beauty and joy, it can literally move heaven and earth. In a world mad with the pursuit of hollow and empty pleasure, Jonathan Edwards's pleasure argument can go a long way. We perhaps can do no better as citizens of heaven than to herald this message of hope and joy, wedded to the truth, as we make our pilgrim journey through this world. We become more than heaven's citizens—we become heaven's ambassadors.

CONCLUSION: PLANTING SEQUOIAS

Edwards extols the virtues of pleasure that, while experienced in the things of the world appropriately enjoyed, is not rooted in this world. Edwards has been talking about a pleasure that breaks in from heaven to earth. The pleasure, sweetness, joy, and delight that Edwards commends to us transcend our world—our world of abundance, as most of us in North America have it, and our world of want and need, as many of our brothers and sisters in such places as North Korea have it. To know that our citizenship is in heaven gives us a place to stand, a perspective on this world that those without Christ do not have. To be a citizen of heaven offers the best vantage point for our temporary citizenship in this world. We can enjoy this world and even contribute to the enjoyment of it by others not in spite of our heavenly citizenship but entirely because of it.

Johann Sebastian Bach always signed his musical compositions, whether commissioned by the church or by kings and nobles for more secular events, with two sets of initials: JSB and SDG. The first set, of course, stands for his name. The second stands for the Latin phrase *Soli Deo Gloria*, meaning "for the glory of God alone." Over the centuries since his death, millions of listeners and musicians have found pleasure in hearing and playing his music. He has left a legacy of joy and beauty. Edwards thought he was only encouraging a handful of colonial New Yorkers as he preached his sermon. But nearly three hundred years later his words inspire and even delight audiences. Bach and Edwards and so many others did not see this world as merely rotting on the vine. Contrary to the saying, they thought it worthwhile to polish the brass as the sinking ship plunges toward destruction and oblivion.

In a rather tongue-in-cheek poem, "Manifesto: The Mad Farmer Liberation Front," Kentucky poet, essayist, and farmer Wendell Berry challenges the don't-polish-the-brass view in a mere two words: "Plant sequoias."[6] How do we live as citizens of heaven? We realize that our hope lies in the world to come. We realize along with the Puritan pastor Jeremiah Burroughs (1599-1646) that while we have great things in hand, we have even greater things in hope.[7] Nevertheless, we also realize that God has made this world and that he has called us to be its stewards. What's more, in bringing heaven to earth—fulfilling our duty as citizens of heaven—we can and should be its greatest stewards. While heavenly-minded, we plant for earthly good.

The giant redwoods, or sequoias, of California and Oregon that are now enjoyed were centuries in the making. They were begun in another era, yet cast their shadow—quite literally— into ours. Wendell Berry, by challenging us to plant sequoias, gently reminds us that we should be mindful of our legacy and of the impact that we may have on life to come. He encourages us to take the long view, to polish the brass on the sinking ship because it is God's ship. We plant sequoias for the generations to come, should Christ delay his return. We seek to bring the beauty and pleasure of enjoying this world to the surface amidst all of the evil and ugliness that vies for attention. We sow beauty so that others may reap beauty, so that they may see and know and love and praise God, the God of all beauty and of all pleasure.

Yet, we cannot ignore the fact that the experience of Christians around the world is not alike. Not everyone can enjoy the concertos of Bach. Not everyone can look past the evil and the ugliness.

Again we can learn from Edwards. His life was not all that charmed, as we saw in Chapter One. His fellow colonials also knew hardship. They experienced high infant mortality, were defenseless in the face of disease, and had little of the creature comforts we take for granted in the modern world. Edwards experienced self-doubt and even rejection. In spite of it all, he could talk of pleasure and joy, sweetness and delight—all because he knew what it meant to be a citizen of heaven. Most western Christians, especially in our North American context, should marvel at that. We should also marvel at, and be humbled by, the resolve and example of our brothers and sisters in places such as North Korea, our fellow citizens of heaven who are denied citizenship in the country in which they live and daily face extreme persecution. Or our brothers and sisters in the underground church in China, facing severe hardships. We should marvel at the sacrifices of our brothers and sisters in Christ in faraway places, far from the comforts of life taken for granted in developed nations.

A group of Christians in Africa are not called Christians by those around them. Instead they are called the people who sing. When someone wants to join their church, they say, "I want to sing." In the midst of very difficult lives full of pain and suffering, poverty and hardship, they sing. They sing from hearts full of joy in Christ. We should tune our hearts to hear such singing. We should marvel at the beauty of their song.

Paul, too, knew what it meant to be in a time of need. And

in those times his heavenly citizenship buoyed him and anchored him. He could turn his sorrow into joy because he knew true reality. The truth is, whatever context we find ourselves living in, it is difficult to bring heaven to earth because, as we have been pointing out, we're plagued either with longing to escape this world or with becoming too fixated on this world. Both perspectives miss out on the privileges of our citizenship in heaven. Our heavenly citizenship affords us the privilege of seeing this world differently, the way God intended it to be seen—a world that is full of beauty and joy and pleasure—a world that has honey. As Edwards rightly says, we should become Christians merely for the pleasure of it.

A heavenly citizenship not only brings high privileges—it also comes with weighty responsibilities. In the next several chapters we'll explore our responsibilities as citizens of heaven living on earth. In the meantime let's enjoy our privileges and enjoy the pleasures of this world. And let's do it so others may see.

4

BUT TO ACT JUSTLY

How unsuitable it is for us,
who live only by kindness, to be unkind!

JONATHAN EDWARDS

THE PAST HISTORY OF Europe's "Christianizing" of the Americas is a mixed bag. Some things should be applauded in those early efforts, but others are worthy only of repentance. In this last category is the missionary zeal in bringing Christianity to Cuba. The Spanish conquistadors, led by Diego Velasquez, met resistance by the native Taino Indians. And so the leading rebels were rounded up and summarily burned at the stake. They were given a chance to repent of their sins and become Christians just before the flames that would take their lives were ignited. Become a Christian, they were told, and they would enter heaven when they died.

Hatuey, one of their chiefs, asked if there would be Spanish Christians in heaven. He was really asking if there would be people like his captors and executioners in heaven. They replied yes, and added that if Hatuey became a Christian he could join them. When he heard that, he said flatly that he had no desire whatsoever to go there. As legend has it, he uttered these last words on February 2, 1512, as he was prepared for the stake: "If Christians [such as you] go to heaven, then I certainly do not want to go there."[1]

The Puritans who settled New England at times fared only marginally better than the Spanish conquistadors. But sometimes they fared much better. One of those times came in the work of Jonathan Edwards among the Mohican, Mohawk, and Brotherton Indians of Stockbridge, Massachusetts, Jonathan Edwards's home and congregation from 1750-1758. Long before he went to Stockbridge, however, Edwards would chastise his New England ministerial colleagues and his parishioners for not doing more for New England's Native Americans, for being poor ambassadors of the gospel of Jesus Christ.

The colonials, Edwards thought, were too caught up in their own advancement to look after the needs and rights of the Native Americans. Their push for their own agendas led them to turn a blind eye to the needs of their neighbors. They neglected their "deeds of charity," as he would put it, and so their gospel witness came off flat and stale. Like Hatuey, many of the New England Indians likely thought that if heaven was populated with such people, they simply preferred not to go there.

Edwards would have quite a bit to say on these matters. A Christian, he would tell his congregation at Northampton, should be "much in deeds of charity," realizing that such a calling is the responsibility of our heavenly citizenship. In the previous chapter we touched on the *privileges* of our heavenly citizenship. We saw how Edwards calls us to enjoy and take pleasure in the beauty and sweetness of our world. We also saw how such living can be a powerful magnet for the gospel, as beauty poignantly speaks to God's presence in this world and his goodness to his creatures. Now we'll see how living out the *responsibilities* of our heavenly citizenship can also be a powerful magnet for the gospel. We'll also see, by contrast, how neglecting our duties can sadly, even tragically, drive people away from Christ and from heaven.

DOING GOOD

Edwards uses the phrase "Much in Deeds of Charity" as a title for a sermon he preached in Northampton in 1741.[2] In the sermon, Edwards also uses the phrase as shorthand for encompassing the so-called "Second Table" of the Ten Commandments. He was borrowing from a rich tradition that saw the Ten Commandments as having two major divisions: laws that orient our vertical relationship with God and laws that govern our horizontal interactions in our various social relationships. The Law, in total, governs every sphere of our lives, both in terms of our relationship with God and in terms of our relationships with one another.

Early in the sermon, Edwards tells us that if we wish to be successful Christians, we must not only pursue our relationship with God in the secret and private acts of piety, such as prayer. "We must also," he challenges, "abound in second table duties, and particularly in deeds of charity or works of love." As Christ commanded, we must love God and love our neighbor (Matt. 22:34-40). In fact, we demonstrate our love for God *by* our love for our neighbor.

Like the New England colonials, American evangelicals

have had a spotty record when it comes to doing deeds of charity, especially over the last century. Evangelicals entered the twentieth century with a robust record of social action. Historians of the great revivals in the 1800s have shown how those revivals led to a great deal of social action for such worthy causes as the urban poor, child labor, and women's rights. But at the turn of the century some significant theological shifts occurred. The early years of the 1900s witnessed the rise of the social gospel movement, which confused social regress with sin and social progress with salvation. In the process, the message of the gospel became distorted.

In the hands of the leaders of this movement, Jesus came to be more and more viewed as the hope of social progress, his death became the symbol of rebellion against the establishment, and his resurrection became the hope of the socially marginalized. The Gospel narratives do show Christ as caring for the poor and needy, as picking up the banner of the Old Testament ethic of caring for the widow and the orphan, the social outcasts who had been pushed aside. But the tragedy of the social gospel movement is that Jesus and his work on the cross came to be viewed *only* this way. As a reaction to this movement, many conservative Christians, known in the early decades of the twentieth century as fundamentalists, began to shy away from engaging in social work and grew lackluster in their efforts to be "much in deeds of charity."

By the middle of the twentieth century, the performance of conservative Christians in this arena drew the criticism of Carl F. H. Henry and his blistering but most necessary book, *The Uneasy Conscience of Modern Fundamentalism*. In a word, Henry demonstrated that we had lost our presence in the world, we had ceased to be the salt and light that Christ called us to be. He indicted us when he said, "We have become the model priest and Levite, bypassing a suffering humanity." Henry took the Parable of the Good Samaritan and hurled it at the feet of the twentieth-century church.[3]

Henry's book heralded a return to seeing the full-orbed nature of Christian discipleship. We must become fully engaged in, not withdrawn from, the world. Henry told us that to live the Christian life, we must pursue both tables of the Law—we must love God and love our neighbor, even if, as we learn from the Parable of the Good Samaritan, such neighborly love is costly and uncomfortable. But we cannot afford to do otherwise. Sometimes we as contemporary Christians have followed Henry's urging, and sometimes we have been negligent. Regardless, we could all do better, and Edwards makes a compelling case for us to live as full disciples.

The social gospel movement of North America or even the more recently felt liberation theology in South America stands as a warning sign not to veer off course as we proclaim the gospel and choose to be "much in deeds of charity." Engaging in social concerns can eclipse the proclamation of the gospel, but it doesn't necessarily have to. We can avoid running aground of such dangers. But we also need to steer clear of a myopic vision of Christian discipleship that keeps our hands clean. We have the second table of the Law to follow.

Beyond the fear that we'll distort the gospel there might be another reason that works against our efforts in deeds of charity, love, and care for the poor and needy. We might simply give up on righting injustices in a world that seems to be so unjust. In heaven, "justice [will] roll down like waters, and righteousness like an ever-flowing stream" (Amos 5:24). For now, justice trickles, and injustice gushes, and righteousness is all but dried up, and unrighteousness rolls in wave after wave. We are overwhelmed by the task.

To be sure, a final reckoning is coming, a day when all will be set right. But that doesn't mean that we should fail to stand against injustices in the interim. In fact, we can put a new twist on Edwards's words from his sermon "Heaven Is a World of Love." There he told us, "As heaven is a world of love, so the way to heaven is the way of love." In this present context he just might say that since heaven is a world of justice, those who are making their way there should demonstrate justice in their lives and actions. Those on their way to heaven should bring heaven to earth by standing up for justice in an unjust world. Edmund Burke said famously, "The only thing necessary for the triumph of evil is for good men to do nothing."

OUR DUTY

Edwards took Acts 10:4-6 as the text for his sermon "Much in Deeds of Charity." After looking at Cornelius, he proceeds to marshal example after example of biblical characters who modeled deeds of charity. He even looks to the examples of his own day in the lives of August Hermann Franke (1663-1727) and George Whitefield (1714-1770). Franke, among other philanthropic works, built an orphanage in Halle, Germany. "God has wonderfully," Edwards tells his congregation, "smiled upon it." Whitefield, too, built an orphanage, in Georgia. In fact, while he was crisscrossing the colonies during the revivals of the Great Awakening (1740-1742), he not only proclaimed the gospel but also raised money for the orphanage and highlighted the need for such acts of love. Edwards uses both Franke and Whitefield as flesh-and-blood examples for his congregation to follow.

Edwards then turns from those examples to his own congregation. What better way to show gratitude for what God has done for them, he asks, than "to abound in deeds of love?" He continues, "What does it signify to pretend to be thankful and yet to neglect our second table duties?" Loving God requires that we be "much in deeds of charity."

By far this wasn't his only sermon on the subject. He also found an obligation for "The Duty of Charity to the Poor," the words of another sermon title, on Deuteronomy 15:7-11.[4] There God commands his people to care for the poor and destitute, to give freely, not smugly, and not grudgingly. So the text concludes in verse 11, "You shall open wide your hand to your brother, to the needy and to the poor, in your land." Edwards draws this clear conclusion as his doctrine for the sermon: "It is the absolute and indispensable duty of the people of God, to give bountifully and willingly for supplying the wants of the needy."

Christians are especially obligated because of all that God has done. First of all, we understand that humanity is made in the image of God. There is an inherent dignity abiding in all humanity that demands that we deal with people differently than our culture might have us deal with them. In the developed countries of the West we tend to value people by their economic contribution. The rich are esteemed more than the poor. And we as Christians are not always immune to such cultural pressures. See James 2:1-13 for an example from the early church. Unfortunately, we succumb to ranking people and their significance by their bank accounts. The truth is that all, rich and poor alike, are made in the image of God, are eternal beings, and are of supreme value. A selfish spirit that neglects charity is, Edwards informs us, "more suitable for wolves, and for other beasts of prey, than for human beings."

C. S. Lewis, as only his imagination could, once called upon us to think of all the human beings that we see, even the lowliest according to social custom, as they truly are, to peel back the layers of flesh, seeing our fellow human beings as eternal beings. Even a momentary glimpse would send us reeling. It would forever change the way we think of one another. It would eternally change the way we understand what it means to be human. "There are no *ordinary* people," he said, adding, "You have never talked to a mere mortal." All human beings are eternal beings, made in the image of God. Class, race, status, or any other marker that we may set up for determining value and significance simply crumbles when we grasp what it truly means to be human.[5]

Christians are ultimately obligated to help the poor and needy because of God's grace, freely poured out on our hearts. We must consider, Edwards exhorts us, that God freely gave us his Son. In response we should readily hand over whatever we can for those in need; we should quickly seek "the relief of a poor neighbor without grudging." Edwards concludes, "How unsuitable it is for us, who live only by kindness, to be unkind!"

Edwards proceeds to chastise us for "pretend[ing] to be the followers of Christ." He adds, "What will it signify to pretend to be Christians, and at the same time live in the neglect of those rules of Christianity which are mainly insisted on in it?" We can't profess to be Christians, in other words, and neglect living like Christians. If we profess to be Christians, we must be "much in deeds of charity." But we don't always live up to our profession, a fact that is not lost on Edwards as he meanders through his sermon. He continues by raising and answering objection after objection—in his day, sermons were somewhat like an Olympic event in logic. But all of the objections fall, leaving the Christian with the obligation to be charitable to those in need.

Edwards admits that this is a "difficult duty," that it "is very contrary to corrupt nature, to that covetousness and selfishness of which there is so much in the wicked heart of man." He also admits that sometimes such duties require that we sacrifice. Yes, it is difficult. But it is also necessary: "It is mentioned in the New Testament as a thing so essential, that the contrary cannot consist with a *sincere* love to God. 1 John 3:17-19." Edwards didn't just preach on being "much in deeds of charity"; he modeled it.

HELPING JUSTICE ROLL DOWN

They were savages. The devil, it was reported, sucked their blood. They were headed, many held, for the destruction for which they were well-designed and made. Of whom were they speaking? The Native Americans who populated New England during the decades of Puritan settlement. And for a span of seven years these were Edwards's congregation.

The first generation of Puritans actually related quite well with the Native Americans. They even managed to see many converts, whom the colonials called "praying Indians." Missionary societies were formed in Britain to send aid, and John Elliott set about translating the Bible in one of the native tongues, Algonquin.

But it wasn't always so good. Edwards himself soon realized that his fellow colonials not only neglected their duty of evangelizing Native Americans—they at times treated them harshly and unjustly. Edwards blew the whistle on his colleagues for their injustice, both in sermons and in his letters coming from his years at Stockbridge (1750-1758). He also worked to undo such injustices as he lived among various Native Americans, mostly Mohicans, nestled along the Housatonic River in the town of Stockbridge, Massachusetts.[6] One study has shown that land was greedily grabbed up from the time of Stockbridge's settlement until 1750, and again from 1758 until the late 1790s when the Mohicans, now without any land, were "removed" first to New York and then to their present-day home in Wisconsin. In the intervening years from 1750-1758, however, such unjust transactions simply weren't taking place. And these were the years when Edwards held the post of pastor.

One time in 1751 he was invited to speak for a rather auspicious occasion, the signing of a treaty with the Mohawks. The audience included a number of Indian leaders, and the English were well represented by Massachusetts's governor, legislators, and prominent clergy. Edwards took advantage of the occasion to preach the gospel, but he couldn't let slide some stinging criticisms of the English. "The Christian religion teaches kindness and love to all mankind," he boldly proclaimed. But this truth was lost on the English. Edwards even went so far as to speak of the "shameful neglect of the white people," who "have not behaved like Christians." They had neglected the greatest act of kindness and love: proclaiming the gospel. The English hoarded the gospel for themselves, inflicting the greatest cruelty on the Indians that they possibly could.

But then Edwards proceeded to say something that was sure to make the Massachusetts dignitaries sweat, if they weren't already. We can almost see them adjust their collars and wipe their brows as Edwards speaks rather plainly to the Indians: "Many of the English and Dutch are against your being instructed. They choose to keep you in the dark for the sake of making a gain of you. For as long as they keep you in ignorance, 'tis more easy to cheat you in trading with you." The economic injustice was another form of cruelty. Edwards shared similar views in a letter with a Londoner of means who was interested in funding American Indian mission work. Edwards let him know what challenges such work faced because of unjust treatment. Edwards wrote candidly: "'Tis true we have traded a great deal, but our trade has been carried on with them in a way that has naturally tended to beget in them a distrust of us, and an aversion to us."[7] The tragedy of such injustice, from Edwards's perspective, was twofold. First, the credibility of the gospel suffered. Second, the English neglected to care for the needs of others as they advanced their own agendas. By not showing love and kindness, they were showing that they really didn't understand what it means to be a disciple of Christ (John 13:35).

Edwards wasn't entirely alone in his revelations of mistreatment and injustice, but he wasn't in the majority either. Nevertheless, he didn't flinch in speaking to the injustices that he saw, and he spoke out for those who couldn't. Many of the Indians could not read or write English, and they had no hope of navigating the courts and the law system of colonial Massachusetts. When they were wronged, they had very little chance of vindication. In addition to his preaching and writing some of his most challenging treatises, such as *Freedom of the*

Will, Edwards would write letter after letter on behalf of various Native Americans wronged in some way or another. In one case in a neighboring town, two Indians were shot and killed as they tried to retrieve their own horses that had been stolen by two Englishmen. When the local officials did nothing, Edwards stepped in. While he could not get the guilty brought to trial, at least he was able to secure indemnity for the bereaved families. Edwards thus added Public Defender to his list of duties.

One of the reasons the Old Testament, and the New Testament for that matter, has so much to say about caring for orphans and widows is that such persons were, in the cultural contexts of the Old and New Testaments, marginalized in their world and left without a voice. How well God's people cared for them and gave them a voice consistently functioned as a barometer of their relationship with and love for God. James 1:27 says it best: "Religion that is pure and undefiled before God, the Father, is this: to visit orphans and widows in their affliction, and to keep oneself unstained from the world."

I find it interesting that James would couple these two together as the marks of true Christianity: caring for widows and orphans and also keeping away from worldliness. Perhaps we can learn something by thinking of the relationship of these two. A wrong kind of worldliness will lead one to be selfish, to ignore or even exploit the weak in the tooth-and-nail fight for the survival of the fittest. But one who understands the responsibilities of a heavenly citizenship, a citizenship that calls us not to abandon but to fully engage our world, will understand exactly the point James makes. The heavenly world breaks into this one when we invert the culture's value system. Heaven breaks in when the needy are cared for and not marginalized, when human dignity stems from the image of God and not from one's economic contribution to society (James 2:1-13 and 3:9-12). Edwards would tell us that without such things one has but a pretend Christianity and not the real thing.

In Edwards's day, those pushed to the margins were the Native Americans. They were his "widows and orphans," sometimes literally, as in the case with the families of the two Indians who were killed by the horse thieves. In the twentieth century, especially in the pre-civil rights, segregated southern states of America, the marginalized were the African-Americans. Among the many who endeavored to give them a voice was John Perkins, the son of Mississippi sharecroppers. In fact, Perkins called his ministry Voice of Calvary, an outreach devoted to the gospel and to social concerns such as voter registration, housing, and health care. When Perkins wanted to tell his story in book form, he took his title from Amos 5:24, *Let Justice Roll Down*—a text famously used by Martin Luther King, Jr. in his "I Have a Dream" speech. Perkins was not waiting for some final reckoning day for injustices to be set right. He sought to bring a little heavenly justice to a world in desperate need. This is how Perkins lives in between.[8]

CONCLUSION

Being a citizen of heaven has great responsibility. It's not too much of a stretch of judgment for us to say that Hatuey's captors, who preached but did not live Christianity, failed to live up to their responsibility. They spoke of heaven, but they acted in such a way that they made heaven a most unwelcome place. My hunch is that none of us will ever burn someone at the stake in the name of Christianity. But in much more subtle ways, perhaps even more by inaction than by action, we leave non-Christians with the thought that if heaven is populated by people like we are, then it's simply not a place worth going to.

Christianity is not true because of the lives of Christians. And heaven isn't the desired destination because it's the home of Christians. Instead, heaven is very much the place where all should desire to go because Christ—the fountain of all love, as Edwards would put it—is there. That is all true. But it is equally true that non-Christians will either see Christ in us or they will not see him. Their vision could be blurred by our misrepresentation, their view of Christ obstructed by our lack of charity and love (Matt. 25:31-46). Or if we are reflecting him in our lives—every aspect of our lives—then they will see Christ and the radiance of his glory in us.

To be a citizen of heaven is to bring heaven to earth, something we saw in the last chapter. This means bringing a bit of justice to an unjust world. It certainly means that through our actions we don't contribute to such injustices. It means that we shelve our personal agendas for the sake of our neighbors. It means that we speak and demonstrate our love even, or perhaps especially, when it's costly and uncomfortable. We can't be pretend Christians. We must live as real Christians. Imagine the impact that we could have in our world if, in the name of Christ, we were "much in deeds of charity."

5

WHILE WE WAIT

It is a matter of great comfort and rejoicing to any person, whatever circumstances he is in, when he can say that he knows that his Redeemer lives.

JONATHAN EDWARDS

Peace I leave with you; my peace I give to you.

JOHN 14:27

I USED TO THINK about writing a book entitled *101 Things to Do While the White-Out Is Drying*. I thought it had potential. After all, a good sixty seconds slips by, sixty seconds that can be irritatingly long. But I waited too long to write that book. Since we could no longer wait for the liquid white-out in the bottles to dry, they gave us instant strips.

Of course, I'm speaking tongue-in-cheek, but only a bit. We are by anyone's count a rather impatient culture, a culture of immediate gratification. We don't like to wait, especially for something good. All of us can remember how the days got so much longer as some significant day such as Christmas or a birthday or some major event like a vacation was on the horizon. Those days and events couldn't come soon enough. And when they did come and go, it seemed like an utter eternity until they came again. Living in between the promise of something and the realization of that promise is one of the hardest things for us to do. We didn't like to wait as children, and most of us haven't become any better at it yet.

But waiting is precisely what we are called to do. Consistently in the lives of the biblical figures there is a lag time between the giving of various promises and the fulfillment of those promises. Joseph was going to be exalted over his brothers. But first he had to be sold into slavery, unjustly imprisoned, and forgotten by his fellow captives. For many passing years, the promise remained unfulfilled. Abraham and Sarah waited. Israel waited for centuries to be freed from bondage in Egypt, only to wander for decades in the desert. And generation after generation had to wait for the Messiah, the promised Deliverer, to come. God told Adam and Eve that the Seed would come. Little did they know that it would take millennia. We, too, are called to wait. We are given the hope of heaven, the hope of perfected bodies, the hope of sinless and unbroken fellowship with God and with one another, but not yet. Now we wait.

There are different ways of waiting. You've observed this in any given waiting room. There's the fidgeter, checking his watch and looking at the clock every thirty seconds and changing positions even more often. There's the efficient waiter, with cell phone and PDA in tow so that not even a nanosecond is lost to unproductivity. And there's the patient waiter, calm and enjoying a moment of quiet, perhaps the only moment of quiet her day will afford.

So, too, there are different ways of waiting for our hope to come, for the fulfillment of all the promises that are ours in Christ Jesus. One way is to leave those promises untapped, solely reserved for the life to come in heaven. Another way is to make a withdrawal on those promises of the life to come for the challenges of this life, to gain perspective on the present by clinging to the promise of the future. This is, according to Edwards, how Job waited. Job, the paragon of patience, waited and waited under dire circumstances. Few, if any, have had to experience the extreme suffering that Job had to endure. There is a reason we speak of "the patience of Job."

If anyone needed perspective, it was Job. Edwards argues that he found it, revealed in the little phrase, "I know that my Redeemer lives" (Job 19:25). Edwards used this text as a sermon he preached in 1740 at Northampton.[1] This was actually a time of waiting for Edwards. The revivals of the middle 1730s in his church had subsided. The revivals in his church, as well as throughout all of the colonies, that would come in the Great Awakening in the next few years were on the brink, but they had not yet come. Edwards had heard rumblings of revival because of the preaching of George Whitefield, and he hoped and longed for revival to come to his church. But for the time being he was living in between.

WHAT'S KNOWLEDGE GOT TO DO WITH IT?

Edwards finds in Job a model for us all, perhaps because Job was a model for Edwards himself. Job's story, though it comes from days of old, is durable, perennial. It has staying power. Edwards observes, "God so ordered it that [Job's] words should afterwards be written in a book by the direction of his own Holy Spirit, viz. in this book where we find them, where they have remained for more than three thousand years, and are more durable than if they were engraven with an iron pen and lead in a rock." The particular words that Edwards refers to are, "For I know that my Redeemer lives." He further draws two implications from these words and the role they play in the narrative of Job's life. First, he points out the privilege of these words, the privilege it is to know that one's Redeemer lives. Second, he emphasizes "how much [Job] values this privilege." Job can speak these precious words with "an air of triumph," even in the middle of desertion and desolation. After Job had lost so much, he was left with his prized possession, the confidence that his Redeemer lives.

Edwards expands the value of this privilege in the doctrine of the sermon: "It is a matter of great comfort and rejoicing to any person, whatever circumstances he is in, when he can say that he knows his Redeemer lives." This little bit of knowledge means everything for Job. This knowledge has everything to do with his time of waiting. This little bit of knowledge becomes all the more meaningful when we consider the type of redeemer that Christ is. Edwards lays this out for us by listing some of Christ's attributes: He is the living, all-sufficient, faithful, unchangeable, and eternal Redeemer. Each of these needs to be unpacked.

Christ is a living Savior, and because he is alive, as Paul tells us, our faith is not in vain (1 Cor. 15:17-20). But not only is he alive, he is the life-giving Savior, he is in fact "the author and fountain of life." Little wonder then that Edwards calls him an all-sufficient Savior, sufficient to restore his people no matter what may come. We also know him to be faithful and unchanging. Edwards contrasts this with our usual experience: "There are many that have formerly appeared to be friends to others that still live, but yet their friendships don't live." Christ, on the other hand, remains faithful to his promises, his mercies never cease, and they never come to an end. Edwards puts it succinctly: "For whom he loves, he loves to the end." And so Christ is an everlasting or eternal Savior. There is no limit, no exhaustion to his work of redemption. He is our Savior now as we live in between.

But Edwards wants to put one more piece of knowledge on the table. Christ is all of these things, but he is also *our* Savior. It's not simply "that we know that Christ is a divine and glorious person, but that he, with all his glories, is ours." We not only know that he lives, "but that he lives for us; that he is risen from the dead and ascended into heaven in our name, and as our forerunner; that he has loved us and died for us." We're not watching from a distance. We are participants. He's not a Savior for others; he's a Savior *for us*. We know him personally and intimately. Job doesn't say *a* Redeemer, or even *the* Redeemer. In his time of trial, it meant everything in the world for him to say, "*my* Redeemer."

TEMPESTUOUS SEAS, SINKING SHIPS, AND ASSURED HEARTS

There is a very practical implication of all of this knowledge that Edwards has been talking about. It brings comfort and rejoicing, no matter the circumstances. In fact, not wanting to leave any stone unturned, Edwards explores no fewer than ten different scenarios in which one might easily be tempted to abandon hope. And these aren't times of minor setbacks or low stakes. Edwards vividly describes times of true despair and despondency, times not unlike those of Job, and times not unlike some of the trials his congregation had faced or might very well face someday. Times that many face while they live in between.

These trials range from spiritual conflict to natural calamities and war, from times of destitution and hunger to times of disease and pain. One chorus of distress and heartache follows another. But Edwards punctuates each with the refrain, "I know that my Redeemer lives," the anchor in the times of trial. So he concludes, "Nothing in their circumstances can keep them from their joy. . . . The building stands strong and unshaken in all storms and tempests." He then adds:

> If he has affliction in the world, and is in the midst of storms, he knows that his Redeemer is above the storms of the world, and can restrain them and quell them when he pleases. 'Tis but for him to say "Peace, be still," and all is calm. If he be tossed on the tempestuous sea, he knows that his Redeemer is in the ship, and therefore knows he can't sink.

We know that God loves us and pities us. He is the God-man, touched with all of our infirmities and frailties and weaknesses. Edwards concludes that Christ as Redeemer has loved us from eternity, still loves us, and will love us throughout eternity. In the tempestuous seas, that is the only knowledge that we need.

As Edwards turns to the application portion of his sermon, he engages in a rather lengthy discussion of assurance, a subject on which he often spoke. The firm conviction ringing through Job's declaration that he *knows his Redeemer lives* reveals an assured heart. Edwards wanted the same for his congregation.

To have an assurance like that of Job would be a great comfort and a great help. Edwards lists some reasons why this is so. First, it will give us boldness in prayer. In fact, this assurance "will make prayer and other duties of religion pleasant to you."

Second, it will also be a great strength against temptation. Third, "It would give you courage to go through difficult duties, and to bear suffering for Christ's sake." Further, "It will greatly draw forth your heart in love to him." Finally, such an assured heart will cause us to engage cheerfully in service to Christ: "It will cause you to do your duty with greater cheerfulness and will draw you on in the way of service, so that you may not only walk but run in the way of God's commandments." All of this flows from knowing that our Redeemer lives.

PEACE ON EARTH NOW

Despite the discordant circumstances, Job found peace. We can find more by Edwards on the subject of peace in his sermon "The Peace Which Christ Gives His True Followers."[2] This sermon, preached in August 1750, comes during a most curious time in Edwards's life. He was voted out of his church on June 22, and he had yet to take his post at Stockbridge.[3] In fact, at this point he hadn't decided what he would do. He was still living in Northampton. And after a few dry weeks of stand-in preachers, his Northampton congregation rather ironically asked him to be the interim pastor.

One could only imagine what Edwards was thinking. He was rejected by his congregation, sure to give even the most sure-footed of us an occasion for self-doubt. He had no idea how he would care for his rather large family of thirteen. What's more, he was gravely concerned for what he took to be a spiritual laxity in his former congregation, a congregation for which he had labored in love for fourteen years. No wonder he preached on John 14:27. At this point in Edwards's life, Christ's final words of comfort could not have been more meaningful or needed: "Peace I leave with you; my peace I give to you. Not as the world gives do I give to you. Let not your hearts be troubled, neither let them be afraid."

Edwards begins by expounding on the text, pointing out the intensely personal interaction of Christ and the disciples at this point in Christ's life. He was about to leave them in a most traumatic and even violent way, and so Christ enters into a "most affectionate and affecting discourse" with the disciples. But it was not a discourse for the twelve disciples only. As Edwards's doctrine for this sermon bears out, when Christ died, he left his peace "as a legacy to all his true saints." Peace is our inheritance. Like Job's confession that his Redeemer lives, this legacy and inheritance is a foundation that will stand even "in times of the greatest uproar." It is not a peace, however, that is yet to come. It is peace now, peace on this earth and in this life. It is peace while we wait.

Edwards was an astute observer of human nature. In the application portion of this sermon, he remarks, "Happiness and rest are what all men pursue." These are worthwhile pursuits, but people tend to look in the wrong place for both. We should not expect to find our happiness or rest in the "vanities" of this world. To such people who do, Edwards offers this invitation: "I invite you now to a better portion. There are better things provided for the sinful, miserable children of men." He continues, "There is a surer comfort and more durable peace: comfort that you may enjoy in a state of safety, and on a sure foundation: a peace and a rest that you may enjoy with reason, and with your eyes open." So Edwards concludes, not unlike his sermon on Job, "In such a state as this you will have a foundation of peace and rest through all changes, and in times of the greatest uproar and outward calamity be defended from all storms, and dwell above the floods. . . . And you shall be at peace."

In these last sentences, Edwards veered quite near autobiography. His world had certainly been shaken up, and he had just come through a calamitous storm—can't you just picture the uproar of the congregational meetings leading up to his dismissal? Edwards had gone through, and was still reeling from, tough times, yet he remained buoyed by the peace of Christ. But there's actually more to it. We not only have the peace of Christ—we have Christ himself. He gives us his peace, and he gives us himself. That is a peace that withstands all assaults.

Edwards concludes the sermon by noting how these "spiritual comforts that Christ offers" are "a surpassing sweetness for the present." They are, however, but a shadow of what's to come:

> They will be to your soul as the dawning light that shines more and more to the perfect day; and the fullest of all will be your arrival in heaven, that land of rest, those regions of everlasting joy, where your peace and happiness will be perfect, without the least mixture of trouble or affliction, and never be interrupted nor have an end.

Edwards's vision of heaven, his vision of life in between, reveals two dynamics at work. The first is that the foretastes of heaven that we enjoy now, such as the peace and rest that Christ gives, are more than enough, more than sufficient for this life. But as the second dynamic brings out, these foretastes also create in us a longing for their fulfillment and consummation. Both facts comfort us as we wait, as we live in between. We have "surpassing sweetness" now. What language can we use to say that we have even more in the life to come?

WEARY PILGRIMS

Given the circumstances that Edwards faced when he preached this sermon, I find it quite odd that he would talk of "surpassing sweetness" in the present. Few of us would likely be able to think of such things, let alone give them voice, let alone give them voice to the very people who had caused the calamity. The only explanation is that Edwards had a future hope that functioned for him as a present reality. He knew well how to live in between, to live now in all of the realities of heaven and the life to come.

Edwards's fellow Puritan, the poet Anne Bradstreet, gracefully articulated the challenges of the pilgrim life a century before Edwards. She had faced hardship. She watched her house burn down with her beloved poems inside. She buried one child, a daughter-in-law, and numerous grandchildren. She endured smallpox as a teenager. Very near the end of her life she wrote one of her most memorable poems, "As Weary Pilgrim, Now at Rest." Through the lines of the poem she unfolds the trials, both physical and spiritual, that had accompanied her life. She expresses the frailties that a hard and difficult life knows all too well. Yet the poem is not a dirge—it is a ray of hope. A hymn of hope for the "rest" and "delight"—her words—that are to come. And so she closes with a look toward her resurrection morning, when the new, "glorious body" shall rise. She exclaims, "Such lasting joys shall there behold." And then she pleads, "Lord make me ready for that day." Her vision of heaven gave her a place to stand in the hardships of her life. She had learned how to wait.[4]

Over the centuries, various Christians have had very difficult times of waiting. For many, like Job, the time of waiting
may be or at least include times of suffering. For many, like
Anne Bradstreet, the time of waiting can be full of hardships
and challenges. In Britain in the 1550s, under the reign of Mary
Queen of Scots, the one whom history dubbed "Bloody Mary,"
scores of devout Christians were imprisoned in the Tower of
London, some tortured and some beheaded or burned at the
stake. They faced excruciatingly intense times of trial.

During World War II, Dietrich Bonhoeffer spent the last
three years of his life imprisoned by the Nazis. He was hanged,
by a direct order from Hitler, at the Flossenbürg Concentration
Camp on April 9, 1945, just days before the Allied forces lib-
erated that camp. His parents had not heard any word of their
son since December. The immediate post-war confusion left
them without any knowledge of his whereabouts. They would
not learn of his martyrdom until the end of July when they happened upon a BBC broadcast of a memorial service held in
London for their son.

In our own day, some suffer greatly for their faith.
Christians in North Korea are not even considered citizens of
their own country.[5] They are limited in what schools they may
attend (the universities are essentially closed to them), what professions they may enter, and where they may live and raise their
families. They have not even a modicum of the rights afforded
their fellow countrymen. They are ostracized by their families
and coworkers. They are viewed as traitors, sellouts to a western God.

Paul tells Timothy, with a clarity that comes from his own
imprisonment and impending death, that "all who desire to live

a godly life in Christ Jesus will be persecuted" (2 Tim. 3:12). While many wait, they suffer persecution.

Others suffer in different ways. The heartache of a prodigal child, an impending job loss in a shifting economy, a spreading cancer mercilessly draining life—all of these and more are extremely difficult circumstances where God may ask us to wait. And in the midst of all of them, Job reminds us that our Redeemer lives, that he is an all-sufficient Savior, an all-sufficient comfort. These three-thousand-year-old durable words have staying power. We, even the best of us, need to admit at times that we are but "weary pilgrims," longing to be at rest.

CONCLUSION

Even without the dire circumstances of suffering, waiting poses its challenges. We grow impatient with ourselves, and we grow impatient with others. We know that spiritual maturity involves time—we just don't always acknowledge that truth. Our natural tendency cuts against waiting, and most of us are not very good at it. The temptation may be to sit and fidget, to waste time while we wait. Even here Edwards has something to tell us.

In a sermon on Paul's admonition "to make the best use of the time" in Ephesians 5:16, Edwards declares, "How little is the preciousness of time considered, and how little sense of it do the greater part of mankind seem to have! And to how little good purpose do many spend their time. There is nothing more precious, and yet nothing of which men are more prodigal." "Hence it appears," Edwards observes, "that time *is exceedingly* precious," too precious to waste. In the next chapter we'll explore some ways that we can make good use of our time even while we wait for our Redeemer.

While we wait for Christ, we also need to keep in mind that we have Christ now. While we wait for our Redeemer, we have our Redeemer now. And because of this we can have peace now. While we wait, we need to hear the words of Christ: "Peace I leave with you; my peace I give to you."

6

IT'S ONLY THE BEGINNING

And doubtless, that which is a part of the happiness of heaven is pleasant and delightful here in this world.

JONATHAN EDWARDS

IN THE OLD CARTOONS the Devil always had a pitchfork, and the angels were always strumming harps. Neither vision got it quite right in portraying what awaits in the eternal state. But somehow those images tend to flood our minds when we think of the afterlife. What will heaven be like? Some think we'll sit on clouds, eat grapes, and listen to harp-strumming angels day after day after endless day.

Others think differently of heaven. They have turned it into one rather posh vacation that lasts quite a bit longer than seven days and six nights. They look to John's account of streets of gold and Christ's talk of preparing "many mansions," from the King James rendering of John 14:2. This view has overcome the temptations of a worldly and temporal materialism by waiting for a heavenly and eternal materialism. The godless have the mansions now, but someday, in that great day of reckoning, we will have the upper hand as we gaze across heaven's vistas from the balconies of our heavenly mansions.[1]

Edwards once preached on the "many mansions" text of John 14:2. His focus in the sermon is not so much on the mansion as our home but on the fact that in heaven we will be with God in the new society. "Heaven is God's house," he tells his congregation, and we should long to be in his house and to dine at his table. Edwards also tells us that it's a big house, adding, "There is room in heaven for a vast multitude; yea, rooms enough for all mankind that are or ever shall be." He closes the sermon by chastising us for thinking of heaven materialistically: "Let the main thing that you prize in God's house be not the outward ornaments of it, [or] an high seat in it, but the word of Christ, and God's ordinance in it." The glory of heaven is God. Edwards won't speculate further about its physical description.[2]

Not only do we like to speculate about the physical aspects of heaven, we also like to speculate about what we'll be doing in eternity. Of course, we have to stretch our minds to think of eternity in the first place. It's like reading a book that never ends. If we take a single grain of sand away from the seashore each day, when the beach is finally depleted, eternity is only beginning. Even in trying to understand, let alone explain the concept of eternity, we're beyond our understanding and capability.

Into all this speculation about heaven and eternity, some sure footing might go a long way. As we have been seeing so far, Jonathan Edwards is a good guide to help us find our way. But Edwards doesn't merely paint a picture of what heaven will be like. He uses that picture to tell us what we should be doing now. This life is one small prelude to the life to come. Or at least it should be. A prelude to a symphony includes all of the themes and motifs that will follow in order to give us a taste of what's to come. The prelude isn't the symphony, but it is the symphony in miniature.

In the previous chapter we looked at waiting. This chapter is really part two of that discussion. What we'll find here is not only Edwards's answer to the question, what will I be doing in heaven? We'll also find out what the answer has to do with life on earth. He tells us that we should be practicing now what we will be doing in heaven. In heaven we will be part of a symphony, the grand symphony serving and praising and glorifying God. We have a lifetime to tune up.

THE BEGINNING AND THE END

Edwards, like the authors of Scripture, refers to heaven as a time of rest and a time of work. We know what work is, and we know what rest is. They're not the same. So first we need to get a handle on this irony of our life in heaven. Part of the problem is that when we think of work, we only do so in the context of a post-fall world. Adam and Eve were cultivating and working in the garden before the fall. After the fall they continued to cultivate and work the earth. Only now they did so by the sweat of their brow. After the fall they had to contend with thorns and pesky weeds.

Adam and Eve before the fall serve as good models for us when we think of heaven. In fact, John in his revelation of the new heavens and the new earth invites us to do just that. His invitation comes in the form of the parallels between Genesis 1—3 and Revelation 22:1-5.

First, there is a river, "the river of the water of life" (cf. Rev. 22:1 with Gen. 2:10). There is also "the tree of life" (cf. Rev. 22:2

with Gen. 2:9). And this tree yields fruit (cf. Rev. 22:2 with Gen. 2:9, 16). We have in some ways come full circle.

The opening chapters of Genesis and the closing chapter of Revelation, however, are not a perfect comparison. Two significant contrasts stand out. First, God created "the two great lights," the sun and the moon, not to mention the myriad stars, to illumine his original creation (Gen. 1:14-19). But these objects are unnecessary in the new creation. There God's glory lights up the sky for all to see (Rev. 22:5).

The second contrast outranks it all. The splendor and beauty and harmony of the original creation comes crashing down as Adam and Eve disobey God (Gen 3:14-19). They brought the curse into all that God had made, into their relationship with God and each other, into the sky and trees, into the animals of land and sea, and into the soil—the soil that ran through their fingers as their hands kneaded the dirt. In the garden of life, pain and suffering, decay and death would be the new world order.

Then we come to the new creation. In the middle of his description of this eternal home in Revelation 22:1-5, John says, "No longer will there be anything accursed." What was done by Adam has been undone by Christ. Adam brought the curse upon us and upon creation. Christ took it upon himself and removed it from us and from the groaning creation. We are back to the Garden of Eden, but it is so much better. It's not better because we can be eternal materialists in a luxurious garden. It's better because we will have unbroken fellowship, perfect fellowship, with God and the Lamb. We will sing his praises, we will serve him, and we will reign with him. We will rest from our burden of sin and from toil in a sin-cursed, thorn-infested world. And we will freely do our work of praising and serving God, our work of relishing his beauty and glory. A work that Edwards says is enough to "fill up eternity."

We will have work, just "no striving and no weariness," as Edwards points out. He continues, "Heaven is not a place of labour and travail, but a place of rest, Heb. 4:9. . . . But the rest of heaven does not consist in idleness, and a cessation of all action, but only a *cessation from all the trouble and toil and tediousness of action.*" It is a work free from "unpleasantness . . . grief and care." For now, all of the difficulties in our way bring about a deeply felt weariness. Here's the good news: in heaven work will be without weariness. Paradoxically, work will be "refreshment." It will also be reward, the highest of reward, as we "perpetually behold God's glory and perpetually enjoy his love." This work will be our eternal happiness.[3]

THE SECRET OF HAPPINESS

Edwards found inspiration for this idea in Revelation 22:3, so much so that as a young man in his late twenties he preached on it at Northampton on March 14, 1731.[4] In the sermon he expands on the following doctrine: "The happiness of the saints in heaven consists partly in that they there serve God." Edwards, always one to talk about pleasure and happiness, joy and delight, was thinking of that age-old question, what is happiness? He puts forth a rather philosophical answer: "When the creature is in that state that is most agreeable to the proper perfection of its nature, then it is in its most happy state."

That's his definition of happiness. Now we need to understand what he's trying to tell us.

It's actually not that complicated. We just need to slowly and carefully dissect his words. Perhaps we should begin with an illustration. When is a runner most happy? When is a concert violinist most happy? A teacher? A skilled carpenter? A mother? A father? When they are running, playing the violin, teaching, constructing a flawless piece of furniture, being a mother, being a father. In other words, we are most happy when we are doing what we in our very beings, our very nature, long to do and are designed to do. When we say that someone's a fish out of water or that someone's out of his (or her) element, we're saying that he is not doing what he is skilled at and what he is meant to be doing. We're saying that such persons are headed for frustration and discontent. Fish are happy when they're swimming.

We were made for God. To have fellowship with him. To enjoy the good things from his good hand. To praise him. To bask in his glory. "A creature," Edwards tells us, "should be most happy when it is according to its design." And we were designed for God. Augustine said it long ago in the opening lines of his *Confessions*: "God has made us for himself, and we are restless, until we find our rest in him." We are discontent, troubled, and frustrated. We're fish out of water. We run here and there looking to find some substitute for fulfillment and meaning and happiness. The Old Testament authors called these things idols, cheap substitutes for the real thing. The Old Testament authors, Augustine, and Edwards all knew the secret to happiness long before the self-help books flooded the market. We are most happy when we are doing and being what God created us to do and to be.

BEING ALL THAT WE CAN BE

As Edwards develops the sermon, he fills in the picture of how we can be and how we can do all that we were meant to be and to do. In short, we were created to praise and to serve God. When we hear this, our response is to cheer and to celebrate. But there's more. For Edwards the route to praising and enjoying God involves service. We were created to serve God. Now the cheering subsides. We don't like to serve. We much prefer to be served. But let's see how Edwards handles this.

Here's a summary of what he's saying:

• We were created to enjoy God. We enjoy God by serving him.

• We were created for happiness. We find happiness in serving God.

Again, let this insight sink in for a while. We don't often think of serving as making us happy. Instead we think we're happy when we are the ones being served. Nevertheless, Edwards offers three reasons why this paradox is true. First, we were not created to be idle but to be active. Athletes don't like to sit on the bench; they want to be in the game. Second, we were created for a certain kind of action. No coach puts his star running back on the defensive line. Third, we were created for the particular action of serving God. "When man serves God," Edwards informs us, "he acts most according to his nature." It is "a most excellent action," an action of true happiness. A smile fills the face of a running back when the coach signals plays that use his abilities.

Some of the most contented individuals in the affluent cultures of the western world are not at the top of the ladder. The unseen and unappreciated workers of our culture are sometimes the happiest. The paradox of Edwards's sermon is true: there is happiness in serving, and there is ultimate happiness in serving God.

Edwards fleshes this out even more as the sermon unfolds. We were designed for this action of service because it is one way for us to express our gratitude for all that God has done. He has created us, which is enough. But he has also redeemed us, which is beyond all that we can fully comprehend. Edwards puts it this way: "[The saints] will see that all the service which they can render to him is but a small recompense for the great redemption."

Then Edwards completes the circle of the paradox. Our service is indeed our opportunity to glorify God. As we glorify him, we are being all that we were meant to be and doing all that we were meant to do. We are, in a word that only Edwards could invent, "happified."

SO NOW WHAT?

Toward the end of his sermon "Serving God in Heaven," Edwards turns to the application. His first point is a basic one: when we understand that we were made to serve God, which means we were made to praise him, we can begin to understand what we will be doing in heaven. Edwards avoids getting caught up in physical descriptions of heaven and instead focuses on describing our activity. Our chief task will be to praise God. He tells us that we will spend eternity in this work. But that's not all. He also explores what this means for life now. We don't begin that work in eternity. We begin it now. We will spend eternity praising God. We should practice now.

Edwards tells us that those whose "hope" is heaven should

work now. We shouldn't be idle; we shouldn't be lazy or lack-luster in our service. Pastor Edwards put it like this:

> Is not the consideration of incessant activity in God's service [by the saints in heaven] sufficient to make you ashamed of your dullness and sluggishness in God's service, your drowsiness in God's worship, your coldness in prayer and in attendance on ordinances, and sleepiness in hearing of sermons, and that you are no more watchful against sin and diligent in doing good in your day?

Edwards also rebukes us for thinking of serving God as a bondage, for thinking of living the Christian life as a drudgery. The saints are serving and praising God; all the while "they enjoy the best and most desirable liberty." The problem is that we, just like the wicked, "have not right notions of happiness." Our happiness should come in praising and serving God. All else falls short.

Edwards closes this sermon with what gets at the heart of this book. He tells us, "The heavenly state is that which God's infinite wisdom has contrived for happiness." Then comes the finale: "And doubtless, that which is a part of the happiness of heaven is pleasant and delightful here in this world. A life of fervent serving of God is a pleasant life." This is Edwards's vision, his contagious vision, of living in between. Heaven is happiness, but not an exclusively future happiness. It's happiness now.

YES, BUT HOW?

So far we've been looking at Edwards's sermon "Serving God in Heaven" on Revelation 22:3 from 1731. A few years later, in 1734, he preached a very similar sermon on Revelation 14:2. In this later sermon he offers help in experiencing pleasure and enjoyment and happiness in this life. He runs through some of the same motivators he stressed back in 1731, such as the love of God and gratitude for the work of redemption. He adds one more to the mix: humility.

In order for us to praise God aright, which is how we serve him, which in turn is how we find fulfillment, we must recognize his glory. And in order to recognize his glory, we must be humble. In fact, this recognition starts us on a beautiful upward spiral. Humility enables us to see the glory of God, and seeing the glory of God takes us to deeper levels of humility, which enables fuller and deeper glimpses of God's glory. Edwards observes, "It is humility only that will enable us to say from the heart, 'Not unto us, not unto us, O Lord, but unto thy name be the glory' [Ps. 115:1]." He continues, "The humble person admires the goodness and grace of God to him. He sees more how wonderful it is that God should take such notice of him, and show such kindness to him, that is so much below his notice."[5]

We don't typically enjoy thinking of ourselves as below or as not worthy of something. In fact, we often think we *deserve* far more than we do. True humility consists in seeing the greatness and grandeur of God and taking an appropriate estimation of ourselves in light of him. It is a moving off of ourselves as the reference, a humanity-centered perspective, and a moving toward God as the reference, a God-centered perspective and worldview. Edwards refers in this sermon to the "grace of humility." Humility does not come naturally. It comes by grace, and it is a grace—a supernatural action, a piece of heaven breaking into this world.

Pride keeps us from serving and praising God. It keeps us from attributing to him the praise and glory for all that we accomplish and even all that we experience. It keeps us from expressing our deep gratitude for all God has done for us. It even hinders our love for him. Pride also keeps us from serving others, from giving due praise to the accomplishments of others, from expressing gratitude to others, and even from loving others. In heaven, humility will be perfected. For now, it ebbs and flows. Cultivating humility goes a long way in learning how to serve and praise God now.

Growing in humility is one way to enjoy the happiness of heaven now. Realizing that we are not alone is another. Edwards speaks of the church as one grand "society joined by grace." Many members of this society have already made their way to heaven, taking their places in the perfect chorus of praise and work of service. Theologians of the old days referred to this as the "church triumphant," the church in heaven, as opposed to the "church militant," the church on earth. Edwards reminds us that we are all one, that we as the church on earth should be employed in the same work as the heavenly church. John gives us a vision of this chorus in Revelation 5:9-14. Edwards wants us to literally tune up now for singing God's eternal praises.

Edwards once said that when he imagines people at their happiest, he sees them singing. When they sing, they are in harmony. When they sing, they do so from joyful hearts. He put such an emphasis on singing that he hired music teachers from Boston to train his Northampton congregation to sing. At one point he was trying to hire a teacher to make it all the way out to Stockbridge to teach his congregation of Mohawks and Mohicans how to sing better.

The truth is, we all need to learn to sing better, and not in terms of musical technique. We need to join in with the opening line of Robert Robinson's hymn, asking God, the "Fount of every blessing," to tune our hearts, sometimes dull and listless and "prone to wander," to sing his praises. In fact, consider how the first stanza unfolds:

Come, Thou Fount of every blessing,
Tune my heart to sing thy grace;
Streams of mercy, never ceasing,
Call for songs of loudest praise.
Teach me some melodious sonnet,
Sung by flaming hearts above;
Praise the mount! I'm fixed upon it,
Mount of God's unchanging love.

As members of the one society joined by grace, we are part of the chorus of praise now resounding in heaven. We contribute our own voice to that chorus, or at least we have the privilege of doing so. Edwards calls on us to enjoy that privilege. And as we do, we'll just be getting started.

Edwards also helps us to enjoy the happiness of heaven by reminding us that God offers foretastes of heaven. As we serve and praise God, we experience the joy and comfort, the glory and happiness to come. In heaven all of this will be perfected. But we can have glimpses and foretastes now. We have an inheritance laid up in heaven. But we can make withdrawals on our account.

As a final way for us to enjoy heaven now, Edwards makes a rather intriguing point regarding redemption. He observes, "The work of redemption is that for which the saints in heaven do chiefly praise God." He adds, "But this work has been wrought here, among us in this world." Christ became flesh in this world. He lived and died and rose again in this world. The world is the theater for God's grand work of redemption, and this world should also be the theater for humanity's praise. Edwards frames it this way: "Shall heaven be filled with praises for what was done on earth, and shall there be no praises on earth where it was done?" "Streams of mercy," flowing from the cross standing on earth's soil, indeed "call for songs of loudest praise."

CONCLUSION

Knowing that we will be perfected in our love for and praise to and enjoyment of God in heaven should only instill in us a desire to be there. It should, in the words of Edwards, "make us long for heaven." It should also make us long to bring this future activity of heaven to earth now. This life is a prelude for the grand, eternal symphony to come.

We started this chapter by asking what we will be doing in heaven. We found the answer in seeing that we will be praising and serving God. We also found that we can and should begin now. "Doubtless," Edwards tells us, "that which is a part of the happiness of heaven is pleasant and delightful here in this world." Doubtless he's right.

7

MEETING THERE
AT LAST

*'Tis of infinitely more importance to have the presence
of an heavenly Father, and to make progress
towards an heavenly home.
Let us all take care that we may meet there at last.*

JONATHAN EDWARDS

JONATHAN EDWARDS was not only a great philosopher, theologian, and pastor. He was a loving husband and father. He and his family experienced times of great joy and times of deep trial. One of those trials came in 1753 when his daughter, Esther Edwards Burr, the wife of Aaron Burr, Sr., and the mother of Aaron Burr, Jr., America's third vice president, was greatly ill. She had married and was with Burr in Newark, New Jersey, where he pastored and served as the president of Princeton University. Many miles separated daughter from parents, who were in Stockbridge, Massachusetts. So they did the only thing they could—they wrote her a letter.

Among Edwards's literary legacy is a rich source of material revealing the Edwards behind-the-scenes, his letters to friends and family. Among these, there are many letters to Esther and her letters in reply. In this correspondence we see the bonds of love that flourished in the Edwards family. We see Jonathan Edwards as husband and father, gently shepherding his family. In fact, we see that the behind-the-scenes Edwards is but a mirror image of the public Edwards. He shares the same ideas in his family letters as he does in his sermons. Not surprisingly, Edwards uses the occasion of Esther's illness and her recovery to talk about the Christian life and about heaven.

As we have seen in previous sermons, he challenges her to "labor while you live to serve God and do what good you can." He then assures her that even though she is separated from her parents by a great distance, "'Tis of infinitely more importance to have the presence of an heavenly Father." He tells her that it is of infinite importance "to make progress towards an heavenly home." And he tells her, "Let us all take care that we may meet there at last." Edwards desired for his children the same thing that he desired for his congregations in New York City, Northampton, and Stockbridge: that they all take part in the grand reunion in the future, that they all meet in heaven at last. It was also his desire that this vision of heaven spur them all on as they made their way to their heavenly home.[1]

Grief would come to Esther and to the entire Edwards family in but a few short years. In 1757 illness would take the life of her beloved companion and husband. The trustees of Princeton looked to Burr's father-in-law, Jonathan Edwards, to assume the office of president. Edwards conceded and made the journey from Stockbridge to Princeton in the early winter months of 1758. Jonathan and Sarah and their few remaining unmarried children would reunite with Esther and her two children at Princeton. Within the first few weeks of his arrival, Edwards took a smallpox inoculation, from which he contracted "a secondary fever." After an intense but short period of suffering—near the end his throat grew so enclosed that "he could not possibly swallow a sufficient quantity of drink"— Edwards died on March 22, 1758.[2]

Esther partook of the same inoculation. Later she too died of fever, on April 7, 1758. She was twenty-seven, leaving behind two small children. Sarah Edwards, now a widow, planned to raise her two orphaned grandchildren.

Sarah was not at Princeton when her husband died. She had remained in Stockbridge to settle their financial matters while he had gone on to prepare the house for her. He made the trek in the midst of winter, at the bequest of the Princeton Trustees, and it was thought that Sarah should wait to travel until the spring months when the journey would be more agreeable. Jonathan's dying thoughts, however, were focused on Sarah and their "uncommon union." He tenderly said, "Give my kindest love to my dear wife, and tell her that the uncommon union, which has so long subsisted between us, has been such a nature as I trust is spiritual and so will continue forever."[3]

Sarah's plans to raise Esther's children never came to pass. In the fall of 1758 she contracted dysentery, then died on October 2. The Edwards clan was beginning to meet in heaven at last.

Both in life and in death Edwards teaches us how to live the pilgrim life. He teaches us that as we make our way to heaven we should serve God and do what good we can. He teaches us that we should long for our heavenly home and that we should enjoy the foretastes of that home now. Edwards also teaches us what it means to die in the Lord—that those who die in the Lord are blessed and that their "deeds follow them" (Rev. 14:13).

Edwards's "deeds" would include his family, his congregations, and his writings. When Jonathan died, Sarah could write
to her daughter, "O what a legacy my husband, and your father,
has left us." In this last chapter we'll consider two more sermons that round out Edwards's vision of heaven on earth. The
first speaks to those who are grieving after the loss of a loved
one. The second portrays our life as a journey home to heaven.

FOR THOSE LEFT BEHIND

In the middle of his Gospel account, which overflows with
demonstrations of the deity of Christ, John offers a most
poignant portrayal of Christ's humanity. Jesus weeps as he
stands among the mourners for his friend Lazarus (John 11:35).
He is our High Priest, sympathetic to our weaknesses and
struck by our frailty (Heb. 4:14-16). Because of Christ's death
on the cross, death has lost its sting. It is a conquered enemy. As
the Puritan John Owen put it, Christ's death was the death of
death. We know that for those who die in the Lord, death is but
the beginning of their rest in heaven. Yet for those left behind,
the sting of loss is all too real. We see not the death of death,
but we see death in all of its ugliness and repugnance. We stand
at the graveside and weep.

Martin Luther, the great reformer, knew all too well the
sting of death. He and his beloved wife Katy lost both an eight-
month-old daughter, Elizabeth, and a thirteen-year-old daughter, Magdalena. As his "Little Lena," as Luther affectionately
called her, was placed in the coffin, Luther remarked to his
friends, "I am joyful in spirit, but sad according to the flesh. The
flesh doesn't take kindly to this. The separation troubles me
above measure." He then captures the conflicting emotion of

losing a loved one in Christ: "It's strange to know that she ... surely at peace and that she is well off there, very well off, and yet to grieve so much."[4]

For Edwards and his contemporaries, life in colonial New England was tenuous. Times of grieving came far too often. The practice of medicine was rudimentary, the germ theory of disease had yet to be discovered, and the rigors of life all conspired to make death an all too frequent reality. Ministers found themselves delivering funeral sermons again and again. On one particular occasion in September 1741, in the throes of the Great Awakening, Edwards preached for the funeral of William Williams, Edwards's uncle and a longtime minister at Hatfield, Massachusetts. Edwards chose Matthew 14:12 and the account of the death of John the Baptist for his text. He titled his sermon "The Sorrows of the Bereaved Spread Before Jesus." And in the sermon he offers hope and comfort for the loved ones left behind.[5]

The disciples of John the Baptist came to tell Jesus what had happened, after Herod maliciously and disgracefully had him executed at Herodias's daughter's wishes (Matthew 14:1-12). This barbaric act nearly cripples John the Baptist's disciples with grief. In this tragic story Edwards finds direction for times of sorrow. Like the disciples of John the Baptist, we are to take our sorrows and our cares and lay them before Jesus. Edwards wisely counsels in the doctrine of the sermon, "When any one is taken away by death, that has been eminent in the work of the gospel ministry, such as are thereby bereaved, should go and spread their calamity before Jesus."

Edwards keenly observes, "The heart that is full of grief wants vent, and desires to pour out its complaint." "But," he con-

a compassionate friend to pour it out before."
such a compassionate friend in Christ. He
rist is such an one, above all others." He is "that
te, all-sufficient Head of the church, and Saviour of
the ᴅᴄ   ᴌat merciful and faithful High Priest, that knows how
to pity the afflicted." "No wonder that John's disciples," Edwards
notes, "when bereaved of their dear guide and teacher, and their
hearts were full of sorrow, came to him for pity."

No wonder that Mary and Martha came to him at the death
of Lazarus either. The expectations of these two sisters "were not
frustrated," Edwards points out, for Christ "was most tenderly
affected and moved at their tears: we are told on one occasion
he groaned in spirit and was troubled, John 11:33. And when he
came to the grave, it is observed, and a special note put upon it,
that he wept, verse 35." Christ, however, came into this world
"not only to shed tears but to shed his blood: he poured out his
blood as water on the earth, out of compassion to the poor, miserable children of men." Edwards assures his audience, his aunt
and his cousins among them, that Christ has the same encouragement and the same compassion for them. Christ has the same
compassion and the same encouragement for us as well.

We may rejoice for the sake of a loved one who is now in
heaven, especially if there was a full life or a time of intense illness and suffering. Other times, when life is cut short, those left
grieving face a terrible loss. They may feel overwhelmed and
even bitter. But no matter what the circumstance may be, death
always leaves a void for those left behind. We may take comfort that someday we will meet them at last, but for now there
is wave after wave of grief. And in these times Edwards gracefully directs us to Christ to tell him of our sorrow, "to tell a com-

passionate Saviour what has befallen" us. And we will find his grace sufficient for all our needs. It's one thing to say this. It takes a deep awareness of who Christ is for it to truly become a reality in our lives.

When Esther Edwards Burr wrote to her father after her husband had died, she could say, "Altho' all streams were cut off yet so long as my God lives I have enough—He enabled me to say altho' thou slay me yet will I trust in thee. . . . O how good is God, I saw the fullness there was in Christ. . . . [He] has been with me in six Troubles and in seven." Sarah also grieved when she heard of her husband's death. "What shall I say? A holy and good God has covered us with a dark cloud," she wrote to her daughter. "But my God lives," she could say in the next breath, "and he has my heart."

Jonathan Edwards's family had learned by his example and by his words of comfort given to others who suffered. When it was his own family's turn to taste sorrow, his counsel did not fail. There is comfort for those left behind. Our sorrow touches our faithful High Priest. Jesus shed his tears, and he shed his blood for us.

Edwards concludes his sermon on the sorrows of the bereaved with one final plea:

> Let us go to Jesus, and seek grace of him that we may be faithful while we live, and that he would assist us in our great work, and that when we are also called hence, we may give up our account with joy and not with grief, and that hereafter we may meet those our fathers, that have gone before us in the faithful labors of the gospel, and that we may shine forth with them, *as the brightness of the firmament, and as the stars for ever and ever.*

We will meet together at the last. For now we look to Christ and seek to be faithful as we make our own journey home.

PILGRIM'S PROGRESS

If John Bunyan hadn't already used the title, "Pilgrim's Progress" would have been a good contender for the sermon that Edwards entitled "The True Christian's Life a Journey Toward Heaven." Edwards used Hebrews 11:13-14 as his text, and he first preached the sermon in 1733 at Northampton. Later he would preach the sermon at Boston, and later still he would preach a condensed version of it at Stockbridge. The sermon was first published in 1765 and has been widely read since. There's a reason Edwards was able to get so much mileage out of this sermon: it in many ways embodies living the Christian life, living in between.[6]

The life in between is the pilgrim life, a theme with a rich history in the Christian tradition. In the Middle Ages, "the pilgrim way" was used to describe literal routes both to the holy city of Jerusalem during the time of the Crusades and to Rome, routes taken throughout the centuries of medieval times. These were great distances at a time when travel proved extremely difficult. Monasteries were constructed along these routes, dotting the hillsides and providing necessary oases of refreshment and rest. Along the way pilgrims would hear heroic stories of those who had gone along before, and they would hear stories of the great things to come when they would finally reach their destination. These stories inspired them on their long, arduous pilgrim journeys.

Martin Luther made his own pilgrimage from his monastery in Germany all the way to Rome. Let's just say that when he got to Rome, he didn't find the salvation he thought he would. He left disillusioned until he found the truth of the gospel, the (re)discovery of the church's treasure of justification by faith alone (*sola fide*).

With the Reformation, the concept of the pilgrim life began to take on new meaning for the church. Perhaps the Puritans in Britain understood this best. Chief among them on this count stands John Bunyan and his beloved book. The allegory of *Pilgrim's Progress* (1678) depicts the circuitous and challenging journey of its memorable main character Christian as he makes his way from the City of Destruction to the glorious Celestial City. Some Puritans even became literal pilgrims, making their way to the new world across the Atlantic Ocean. Edwards is a part of this legacy, and he shows his true heritage in his sermon on the pilgrim life.

Edwards looked to Hebrews 11:13-14 as his text. In this famous chapter we find the heroic stories of those who have made their pilgrim way before us, their testimonies left as markers to the faithfulness of God and the perseverance of his saints. The text, in the fuller context of 11:13-16, declares:

> *These all died in faith, not having received the things promised, but having seen them and greeted them from afar, and having acknowledged that they were strangers and exiles on the earth. For people who speak thus make it clear that they are seeking a homeland. If they had been thinking of that land from which they had gone out, they would have had opportunity to return. But as it is, they desire a better country, that is, a heavenly one. Therefore God is not ashamed to be called their God, for he has prepared for them a city.*

The author of Hebrews in this passage sums up much of

what we have been talking about concerning life in between. We see that these saints lived in between the promise and its fulfillment, that they were citizens of heaven and sojourners on earth, and that God had called them to be faithful pilgrims. We also see how this vision of heaven is precisely what enabled them to live their pilgrim lives. Finally, we see that they are our example.

Edwards unpacks all of this in his sermon. He first reminds us that this life is "a journey or pilgrimage towards heaven." We should travel light. We may enjoy life, "settled in families with desirable friends and relations. We have companions whose society is delightful, and children in whom we see many promising qualifications." This is not our exclusive portion, Edwards reminds us. We ought to possess and enjoy all of these wonderful things as gifts from God. We hold them all, however, with open hands, ready to leave them for heaven.

TRAVELING TIPS

With this perspective, Edwards offers some traveling tips:

1. *We should set our hearts on heaven.* This will help keep us from becoming distracted or too constrained by the pulls and desires of this world. We must always remember that we are travelers.

2. *We seek heaven by taking the proper route: holiness.* Back in Chapter Two we saw that Edwards teaches us that since heaven is a world of love, the way to heaven is the way of love. Now he adds that the way to heaven is also the way of holiness. On one occasion Edwards referred to holiness as "a duty of delight." Here he reminds us that holiness is a journey upstream, traveling against the natural flow of our selfish and

sinful appetites and desires. The way to heaven is the way of holiness.

3. *We must be ready for hard times.* The way can be difficult, this world sometimes a wilderness. This requires that we be prepared and that we be fit for the journey.

4. *We must stay at it.* There are no shortcuts, no stops. We are to begin our journey "early in life," and we must persevere until the end.

5. *We should be making continual progress.* I once had a professor who had a knack for illustrating things. He said some view the Christian life as a roller coaster: one day they're up, the next day they're down. He preferred to liken the Christian life to someone walking uphill with a yo-yo in hand. We might have minor ups and downs, but the ideal Christian life is one of sometimes slow but nevertheless continual progress.

6. *We need to keep our goal in view.* We should eat and drink and enjoy our friends as we make our journey. Again, these are the good things of life that God has given us as refreshment and enjoyment along our way. But they are tokens of the good things to come. We must keep our eyes fixed on the better country, the heavenly country that awaits us.

As the sermon unfolds, Edwards further develops these points. He tells us that "when persons are converted, they do but begin their work." At conversion we have tasted of grace; we "have once tasted of the blessings of Canaan." We should "with utmost diligence" strive after the way of grace, all the while inspired by the reward that awaits us at the end of the journey. We have merely tasted of grace. There is far more to come.

Edwards describes the far more that is to come in ways that

only he can. "How worthy is heaven," he tells us, "that your life should be wholly spent as a journey towards it. To what better purpose can you spend your life?" He continues, "How can you better employ your strength, use your means, and spend your days, than in traveling the road that leads to the everlasting enjoyment of God; to his glorious presence; to the new Jerusalem; to the heavenly mount Zion; where all your desires will be filled, and no danger of ever losing your happiness?"

Edwards re-preached this sermon at Stockbridge to the Mohicans and Mohawks in the winter of 1754. He modified it a bit, deleting some portions while adding others. Toward the end of the sermon manuscript, he scribbled some final observations. He notes that in heaven there is "no sin, no pride, no malice, [no] hating one another, no hurting one another, [no] killing one another . . . no death, no old age, no winter." Instead, he crescendos, heaven is a place where "hearts are full of love" and "full of happiness."[7]

This is his contagious vision of heaven. A vision that he lived throughout his life. A vision that he preached on at Northampton and at the missionary outpost of Stockbridge. A vision that buoyed him and his family in times of trial and sorrow. A vision that had everything to do with life on earth. At the end of his sermon on the pilgrim life, Edwards offers one final exhortation: "Let Christians help one another in going this journey." He also notes that "company is very desirable" on this pilgrimage. We are not alone. We have many, Edwards among them, who have gone on before and point the way for us. Edwards calls us to do the same for others, as we all long for "a more joyful meeting at our Father's house in glory."

CONCLUSION

I mentioned in the Introduction to this book that Edwards is such a good guide for living the Christian life because he so well points us to Scripture and to Christ, just like the author of Hebrews in the opening verses of chapter 12. Life in this world is a pilgrim journey. Along our way we find inspiration in the lives of others, in their testimonies of faithfulness in the midst of suffering and persecution, and in their quest for the better country.

But into this world also came our Savior, who took on flesh and dwelt among us. He experienced persecution and suffering, loss and betrayal. While he was here, he sought to do his Father's will. He spoke of justice in an unjust world. He stooped low to help a suffering and beaten-down humanity. He modeled peace and harmony amidst strife and conflict. He spoke of joy and happiness in a culture of complaint and discontent. He sowed love and life among hatred and death. Christ was heaven on earth. And he has called us to be his disciples.

It is little wonder that the author of Hebrews commands us to "run with endurance the race that is set before us, looking to Jesus, the founder and perfecter of our faith, who for the joy that was set before him endured the cross, despising the shame, and is seated at the right hand of the throne of God" (12:1b-2). Someday we will meet there at last, gathered around the throne.

In the meantime, may we capture this vision of heaven while we live out our lives on earth. It was a contagious vision in the hands of Jonathan Edwards. He has provoked generations to seek the better country of heaven. May we too be contagious as we live out our vision of heaven in our life on earth. What a "joyful meeting at our Father's house" it will be.

APPENDIX:

Heaven Is a World of Love (Abridged)

BY JONATHAN EDWARDS

INTRODUCTION BY STEPHEN J. NICHOLS

Of all the sermons explored in the previous chapters, "Heaven Is a World of Love" seems to capture Jonathan Edwards's vision of heaven on earth the best. This sermon was the final installment in Edwards's sermon series on Paul's exquisite chapter on love, 1 Corinthians 13. The old King James Version word for love was *charity*. So Edwards entitled his series "Charity and Its Fruits." In the first of these fifteen sermons, Edwards declares that love is the sum of all the virtues. The doctrine for that sermon reads, "That all the virtue that is saving, and that distinguishes true Christians from others, is summed up in Christian love." It is love directed to God first and to our neighbors second. It is an active love, one that also results in serving God and serving others. This love and its fruits are the telltale signs of discipleship.

Edwards closes his series by reflecting on 1 Corinthians 13:8-10, the promise of perfected love that awaits us in heaven. He pulls out all stops in describing the glorious future for us in heaven, the world of love. The sermon truly inspires. But as we have seen in the previous chapters, Edwards sought not only to inspire but also to instruct. As he ends this sermon, he reminds us that if heaven is a world of love, then the way to heaven is the way of love.

The late Paul Ramsey, an Edwards scholar at Princeton University, lamented that most who know Edwards know him only as the preacher of "Sinners in the Hands of an Angry God" and not as the preacher of "Heaven Is a World of Love." Edwards had a profound sense of sin and judgment—made quite clear in "Sinners." He had an equally profound sense of the beauty and joy of God, of the glory of heaven, and of the happiness of God's children. He knew the pain and misery of life, and he understood the evil of the human heart. But he also knew of the power of love. He knew the power of a life of love, the power of living on earth as it is and in heaven.

A NOTE ON THE TEXT

Edwards preached this sermon series between April and October 1738. Tryon Edwards, a grandson, first published the sermon series in 1851. His edition has been widely reprinted, available currently as Jonathan Edwards, *Charity and Its Fruits* (Carlisle, PA: The Banner of Truth, 1969). Tryon Edwards's version has sixteen sermons, as he divided the fourth sermon into two. The scholarly edition of the entire sermon series, along with a helpful introduction, is available in *The Works of Jonathan Edwards, Volume 8: Ethical Writings*, edited by Paul Ramsey (New Haven, CT: Yale University Press, 1989).

The original manuscript has been lost. The scholarly edition of the sermon is based on an early nineteenth-century manuscript in an unknown hand that is part of the Edwards manuscript collection at Andover-Newton Theological

Seminary in Massachusetts. It is not known on which manuscript Tryon Edwards based his edition.

The text reprinted here is based on Tryon Edwards's version, with some stylistic and editorial changes. The final paragraph comes from the conclusion of the Paul Ramsey edition. I have abridged the sermon to roughly half of its original length. If it's any consolation to modern readers (and preachers), he likely took more than one service to preach the full sermon.

"Heaven Is a World of Love" is only the tip of the iceberg. Any one of the other sermons offers equal inspiration and instruction for living the Christian life. If this book whets your appetite for more of Edwards, then the references in the footnotes will help you track down the other sermons. Reading Edwards's sermons well repays the effort.

THE SERMON, ABRIDGED
"Heaven Is a World of Love"
Jonathan Edwards

October 1738

1 Corinthians 13:8-10: Charity never faileth: but whether there be prophecies, they shall fail; whether there be tongues, they shall cease; whether there be knowledge, it shall vanish away. For we know in part, and we prophesy in part. But when that which is perfect is come, then that which is in part shall be done away.

From the first of these verses, I have already drawn the doctrine, that that great fruit of the Spirit in which the Holy Ghost shall not only for a season, but everlastingly, be communicated to the church of Christ, is divine love.[1] And now I would consider the same verse (1 Cor. 13:8) in connection with the two that follow it (1 Cor. 13:9-10) and upon the three verses would make two observations. *First,* that it is mentioned as one great excellence of love, that it shall remain when all other fruits of the Spirit have failed. *Second,* that this will come to pass in the perfect state of the church, when that which is in part shall be done away, and that which is perfect is come. . . .

DOCTRINE

Heaven is a world of love.

The apostle speaks, in the text, of a state of the church when it is perfect in heaven, and therefore a state in which the Holy Spirit shall be more perfectly and abundantly given to the church than it is now on earth. But the way in which it shall be given when it is so abundantly poured forth, will be in that great fruit of the Spirit, holy and divine love, in the hearts of all the blessed inhabitants of that world. So that the heavenly state of the church is a state that is distinguished from its earthly state, as it is that state which God has designed especially for such a communication of his Holy Spirit, and in which it shall be given perfectly, whereas, in the present state of the church, it is given with great imperfection. And it is also a state in which this holy love or charity shall be, as it were, the only gift or fruit of the Spirit, as being the most perfect and glorious of all, and which, being brought to perfection, renders all other gifts that God bestowed on his church on earth needless.

And that we may the better see how heaven is thus a world of holy love, I would consider, *first,* the great cause and fountain of love that is in heaven; *second,* the objects of love that it contains; *third,* the subjects of that love; *fourth,* its principle, or the love itself; *fifth,* the excellent circumstances in which it is there exercised and expressed and enjoyed; and, *sixth,* the happy effects and fruits of all this.

I. *The Cause and Fountain of love in heaven.* Here I remark that the God of love himself dwells in heaven. Heaven is the palace or presence-chamber of the high and holy One, whose name is love, and who is both the cause and source of all holy love. God, considered with respect to his essence, is everywhere. He fills both heaven and earth. But yet he is said, in some respects, to be more especially in some places than in others. He was said of old to dwell in the land of Israel, above all other lands; and in Jerusalem, above all other cities of that land; and in the temple, above all other buildings in the city; and in the holy of holies, above all other apartments of the temple; and on the mercy seat, over the ark of the covenant, above all other places in the holy of holies. But heaven is his dwelling-place above all other places in the universe; and all those places in which he was said to dwell of old, were but types of this. Heaven is a part of creation that God has built for this end, to be the place of his glorious presence, and it is his abode forever; and here will he dwell, and gloriously manifest himself to all eternity.

And this renders heaven a world of love. God is the fountain of love, as the sun is the fountain of light. And therefore the glorious presence of God in heaven fills heaven with love, as the sun, placed in the midst of the visible heavens in a clear day, fills the world with light. The apostle tells us that "God is love" (1 John 4:8). And therefore, seeing he is an infinite being, it follows that he is an infinite fountain of love. Seeing he is an all-sufficient being, it follows that he is a full and overflowing, and inexhaustible fountain of love. And in that he is an unchangeable and eternal being, he is an unchangeable and eternal fountain of love.

There, even in heaven, dwells the God from whom every stream of holy love, yea, every drop that is, or ever was, proceeds. There dwells God the Father, God the Son, and God the Spirit, united as one, in infinitely dear, and incomprehensible, and mutual, and eternal love. There dwells God the Father, who is the father of mercies, and so the father of love, who so loved the world as to give his only-begotten Son to die for it. There dwells Christ, the Lamb of God, the prince of peace and of love, who so loved the world that he shed his blood, and poured out his soul unto death for men. There dwells the great Mediator, through whom all the divine love is expressed toward men, and by whom the fruits of that love have been purchased, and through whom they are communicated, and through whom love is imparted to the hearts of all God's people. There dwells Christ in both his natures, the human and the divine, sitting on the same throne with the Father. And there dwells the Holy Spirit, the Spirit of divine love, in whom the very essence of God, as it were, flows out, and is breathed forth in love, and by whose immediate influence all holy love is shed abroad in the hearts of all the saints on earth and in heaven.

There, in heaven, this infinite fountain of love, this eternal Three in One, is set open without any obstacle to hinder access to it, as it flows forever. There this glorious God is manifested, and shines forth, in full glory, in beams of love. And there this glorious fountain forever flows forth in streams, yea, in rivers of love and delight, and these rivers swell, as it were, to an ocean of love, in which the souls of the ransomed may bathe with the sweetest enjoyment, and their hearts, as it were, be deluged with love!

II. *To the objects of love that heaven contains.* Here I would observe three things.

1. *There are none but lovely objects in heaven.* No odious, or unlovely, or polluted person or thing is to be seen there. There is nothing there that is wicked or unholy. "There shall in no wise enter into it anything that defiles, neither whatsoever works abomination" (Rev. 21:27). And there is nothing that is deformed with any natural or moral deformity; but everything is beauteous to behold, and amiable and excellent in itself. . . . All the persons that belong to the blessed society of heaven are lovely. The Father of the family is lovely, and so are all his children; the head of the body lovely, and so are all the members. . . .

2. *They shall be perfectly lovely.* There are many things in this world that in the general are lovely, but yet are not perfectly free from that which is the contrary. There are spots on the sun; and so there are many men that are most amiable and worthy to be loved, who yet are not without some things that are disagreeable and unlovely. Often there is in good men some defect of temper, or character, or conduct, that mars the excellence of what otherwise would seem most amiable; and even the very best of men, are, on earth, imperfect. But it is not so in heaven. There shall be no pollution, or deformity, or unamiable defect of any kind, seen in any person or thing; but everyone shall be perfectly pure and perfectly lovely in heaven. That blessed world shall be perfectly bright, without any darkness; perfectly fair, without any spot; perfectly clear, without any cloud. . . .

3. *In heaven shall be all those objects that the saints have set their hearts upon, and which they have loved above all*

things while in this world. There they will find those things that appeared most lovely to them while they dwelt on earth; the things that met the approbation of their judgments, and captivated their affections, and drew away their souls from the most dear and pleasant of earthly objects. There they will find those things that were their delight here below, and on which they rejoiced to meditate, and with the sweet contemplation of which their minds were often entertained. And there, too, are the things which they chose for their portion, and which were so dear to them that they were ready for the sake of them to undergo the severest sufferings, and to forsake even father, and mother, and kindred, and friends, and wife, and children, and life itself. All the truly great and good, all the pure and holy and excellent from this world, and from every part of the universe, are constantly tending toward heaven. As the streams tend to the ocean so all these are tending to the great ocean of infinite purity and bliss.

The progress of time does but bear the saints on to blessedness. And we, if we are holy, are to be united to them there. Every gem which death rudely tears away from us here is a glorious jewel forever shining there. Every Christian friend that goes before us from this world is a ransomed spirit waiting to welcome us in heaven. There will be the infant of days that we have lost below, through grace to be found above. There the Christian father, and mother, and wife, and child, and friend, with whom we shall renew the holy fellowship of the saints, which was interrupted by death here, shall be commenced again in heaven, and then shall never end. There we shall have company with the patriarchs and fathers and saints of the Old and New Testaments, and those of whom the world was not worthy, with whom on earth we were only conversant by faith. And there, above all, we shall enjoy and dwell with God the Father, whom we have loved with all our hearts on earth; and with Jesus Christ, our beloved Savior, who has always been to us the chief among ten thousands, and altogether lovely; and with the Holy Ghost, our Sanctifier, and Guide, and Comforter; and shall be filled with all the fullness of the Godhead forever. . . .

[III. *To heaven's subjects*, which are the hearts in which it dwells. . . . IV. *Of the principle of love in heaven.*]

V. *The excellent circumstances in which love shall be exercised and blessed, and enjoyed in heaven.* Here I observe ten points.

1. *Love in heaven is always mutual.* It is always met with answerable returns of love that are proportioned to its exercise. Such returns, love always seeks; and just in proportion as any person is beloved, in the same proportion is his love desired and prized. And in heaven this desire of love, or this fondness for being loved, will never fail of being satisfied. No inhabitants of that blessed world will ever be grieved with the thought that they are slighted by those that they love, or that their love is not fully and fondly returned. As the saints will love God with an inconceivable ardency of heart, and to the utmost of their capacity, so they will know that he has loved them from all eternity, and still loves them, and will continue to love them forever. . . .

2. *The joy of heavenly love shall never be interrupted or damped by jealousy.* Heavenly lovers will have no doubt of the love of each other. They shall have no fear that the declarations and professions of love are hypocritical, but shall be perfectly satisfied of the sincerity and strength of each other's affection,

as much as if there were a window in every breast, so that everything in the heart could be seen. There shall be no such thing as flattery or dissimulation in heaven, but there perfect sincerity shall reign through all and in all. Every one will be just what he seems to be, and will really have all the love that he seems to have. It will not be as in this world, where comparatively few things are what they seem to be, and where professions are often made lightly and without meaning; but there every expression of love shall come from the bottom of the heart, and all that is professed shall be really and truly felt. . . .

3. *There shall be nothing within themselves to clog or hinder the saints in heaven in the exercises and expressions of love.* In this world the saints find much to hinder them in this respect. They have a great deal of dullness and heaviness. They carry about with them a heavy-molded body, a clod of earth, a mass of flesh and blood that is not fitted to be the organ for a soul inflamed with high exercises of divine love; but which is found a great clog and hindrance to the spirit, so that they cannot express their love to God as they would, and cannot be so active and lively in it as they desire. Often they fain would fly, but they are held down as with a dead weight upon their wings. Fain would they be active, and mount up, as a flame of fire, but they find themselves, as it were, hampered and chained down, so that they cannot do as their love inclines them to do. Love disposes them to burst forth in praise, but their tongues are not obedient. They lack words to express the ardency of their souls, and cannot order their speech by reason of darkness (Job 37:19). And often, for want of expressions, they are forced to content themselves with groanings that cannot be uttered (Rom. 8:26). But in heaven they shall have no such hindrance. . . .

4. *In heaven love will be expressed with perfect decency and wisdom.* Many in this world that are sincere in their hearts, and have indeed a principle of true love to God and their neighbor, yet lack discretion to guide them in the manner and circumstances of expressing it. Their intentions, and so their speeches, are good, but often not suitably timed, nor discreetly ordered as to circumstances, but are attended with an indiscreetness that greatly obscures the loveliness of grace in the eyes of others. But in heaven the amiableness and excellence of their love shall not be obscured by any such means. There shall be no indecent or unwise or dissonant speeches or actions, no foolish and sentimental fondness, no needless officiousness, no low or sinful propensities of passion, and no such thing as affections clouding or deluding reason, or going before or against it. But wisdom and discretion shall be as perfect in the saints as love is, and every expression of their love shall be attended with the most amiable and perfect decency and discretion and wisdom.

5. *There shall be nothing external in heaven to keep its inhabitants at a distance from each other, or to hinder their most perfect enjoyment of each other's love.* There shall be no wall of separation in heaven to keep the saints apart, nor shall they be hindered from the full and complete enjoyment of each other's love by distance of habitation. They shall all be together, as one family, in their heavenly Father's house. Nor shall there be any want of full acquaintance to hinder the greatest possible intimacy; and much less shall there be any misunderstanding between them, or misinterpreting things that are said or done by each other. There shall be no disunion through difference of temper, or manners, or circumstances, or from various opinions, or interests, or feelings, or alliances. But all shall be united in

the same interests, and all alike allied to the same Savior, and all employed in the same business, serving and glorifying the same God.

6. *In heaven all shall be united together in very near and dear relations.* Love always seeks a near relation to the one who is beloved; and in heaven they shall all be nearly allied and related to each other. All shall be nearly related to God, the supreme object of their love, for they shall all be his children. And all shall be nearly related to Christ, for he shall be the head of the whole society, and the husband of the whole Church of saints, all of whom together shall constitute his spouse. And they shall all be related to each other as brethren, for all will be but one society, or rather but one family, and all members of the household of God.

7. *In heaven all shall have property and ownership in each other.* . . . Divine love rejoices in saying, "My beloved is mine, and I am his." And in heaven all shall not only be related one to another, but they shall be each other's, and belong to each other. The saints shall be God's. He brings them home to himself in glory, as that part of the creation that he has chosen for his peculiar treasure. And on the other hand, God shall be theirs, made over to them in an everlasting covenant in this world, and now they shall be forever in full possession of him as their portion. And so the saints shall be Christ's, for he has bought them with a price; and he shall be theirs, for he that gave himself for them will have given himself to them; and in the bonds of mutual and everlasting love, Christ and the saints will have given themselves to each other. And as God and Christ shall be the saints', so the angels shall be "their angels" (Matt. 18:10). And the saints shall belong to one another, for the apos-

tle speaks of the saints in his days, as first giving themselves to the Lord, and then to one another by the will of God (2 Cor. 8:5). If this is done on earth, it will be more perfectly done in heaven.

8. *In heaven they shall enjoy each other's love in perfect and uninterrupted prosperity.* What often on earth alloys the pleasure and sweetness of worldly pleasure, is, that though persons live in love, yet they live in poverty, or meet with great difficulties and sore afflictions, whereby they are grieved for themselves and for one another. For, though in such cases love and friendship in some respects lighten the burden to be borne, yet in other respects they rather add to its weight, because those that love each other become, by their very love, sharers in each other's afflictions. Each has not only his own trials to bear, but those also of his afflicted friends. But there shall be no adversity in heaven to give occasion for a pitiful grief of spirit, or to molest or disturb those who are heavenly friends in the enjoyment of each other's friendship. But they shall enjoy one another's love in the greatest prosperity. . . .

9. *In heaven all things shall conspire to promote their love, and give advantage for mutual enjoyment.* There shall be none there to tempt any to dislike or hatred; no busybodies, or malicious adversaries, to make misrepresentations, or create misunderstandings, or spread abroad any evil reports, but every being and everything shall conspire to promote love, and the full enjoyment of love. Heaven itself, the place of habitation, is a garden of pleasures, a heavenly paradise, fitted in all respects for an abode of heavenly love. . . . The petty distinctions of this world do not draw lines in the society of heaven, but all meet in the equality of holiness and of holy love. . . .

10. *The inhabitants of heaven shall know that they shall forever be continued in the perfect enjoyment of each other's love.* They shall know that God and Christ shall be forever with them as their God and portion, and that his love shall be continued and fully manifested forever, and that all their beloved fellow-saints shall forever live with them in glory, and shall forever keep up the same love in their hearts which they now have. And they shall know that they themselves shall ever live to love God, and love the saints, and to enjoy their love in all its fullness and sweetness forever. They shall be in no fear of any end to this happiness, or of any abatement from its fullness and blessedness, or that they shall ever be weary of its exercises and expressions, or cloyed with its enjoyments, or that the beloved objects shall ever grow old or disagreeable, so that their love shall at last die away.

All in heaven shall flourish in immortal youth and freshness. Age will not there diminish anyone's beauty or vigor; and their love shall abide in everyone's heart, as a living spring perpetually springing up in the soul, or as a flame that never dies away. And the holy pleasure of this love shall be as a river that is forever flowing clear and full, and increasing continually. . . .

Having thus noticed many of the blessed circumstances with which love in heaven is exercised, and expressed, and enjoyed, I proceed to speak lastly of the sixth point.

VI. *Of the blessed effects and fruits of this love, as exercised and enjoyed in heaven.* And of the many blessed fruits of it, I would at this time mention only two.

1. *The most excellent and perfect behavior of all the inhabitants of heaven toward God and each other.* Divine love is the sum of all good principles, and therefore the fountain whence

proceed all amiable and excellent actions. And as in heaven this love will be perfect, to the perfect exclusion of all sin consisting in enmity against God and fellow creatures, so the fruit of it will be a most perfect behavior toward all. Hence life in heaven will be without the least sinful failure or error. . . .

We know not particularly how the saints in heaven shall be employed; but in general we know that they are employed in praising and serving God; and this they will do perfectly, being influenced by such a love as we have been considering. And we have reason to think that they are so employed as in some way to be subservient, under God, to each other's happiness, for they are represented in the Scriptures as united together in one society, which, it would seem, can be for no other purpose but mutual subservience and happiness. And they are thus mutually subservient by a perfectly amiable behavior one towards another, as a fruit of their perfect love one to another. . . .

2. *The other fruit of love exercised in heaven is perfect tranquility and joy.* Holy and humble Christian love is a principle of wonderful power to give ineffable quietness and tranquility to the soul. It banishes all disturbance, and sweetly composes and brings rest to the spirit, and makes all divinely calm and sweet and happy. In that soul where divine love reigns and is in lively exercise, nothing can cause a storm, or even gather threatening clouds. . . .

Oh! what tranquility will there be in such a world as this! Who can express the fullness and blessedness of this peace? What a calm is this! How sweet, and holy, and joyous! What a haven of rest to enter, after having passed through the storms and tempests of this world, in which pride, and selfishness, and envy, and malice, and scorn, and contempt, and contention, and vice, are as waves of a restless ocean, always rolling, and often dashed about in violence and fury! What a Canaan of rest to come to, after going through this waste and howling wilderness, full of snares, and pitfalls, and poisonous serpents, where no rest could be found! . . .

Every saint in heaven is as a flower in that garden of God, and holy love is the fragrance and sweet odor that they all send forth, and with which they fill the bowers of that paradise above. Every soul there is as a note in some concert of delightful music that sweetly harmonizes with every other note, and all together blend in the most rapturous strains in praising God and the Lamb forever. And so all help each other, to their utmost, to express the love of the whole society to its glorious Father and Head, and to pour back love into the great fountain of love whence they are supplied and filled with love, and blessedness, and glory. And thus they will love, and reign in love, and in that godlike joy that is its blessed fruit, such as eye hath not seen, nor ear heard, nor hath ever entered into the heart of man in this world to conceive. And thus in the full sunlight of the throne, enraptured with joys that are forever increasing, and yet forever full, they shall live and reign with God and Christ forever and ever.

APPLICATION

1. *If heaven be such a world as has been described, then we may see a reason why contention and strife tend to darken our evidence of fitness for its possession.* Experience teaches that this is the effect of contention. When principles of malignity and ill-will prevail among God's people, as they sometimes do through the remaining corruption of their hearts, and they get into a

contentious spirit, or are engaged in any strife whether public or private, and their spirits are filled with opposition to their neighbors in any matter whatever, their former evidences for heaven seem to become dim, or die away. They are in darkness about their spiritual state, and do not find that comfortable and satisfying hope that they used to enjoy.

And so, when converted persons get into ill frames in their families, the consequence commonly, if not universally, is that they live without much of a comfortable sense of heavenly things, or any lively hope of heaven. They do not enjoy much of that spiritual calm and sweetness that those do who live in love and peace. They have not that help from God, and that communion with him, and that near intercourse with heaven in prayer, that others have. The apostle seems to speak of contention in families as having this influence. His language is, "Likewise, ye husbands, dwell with [your wives] according to knowledge, giving honour unto the wife, as unto the weaker vessel; and as being heirs together of the grace of life, that your prayers be not hindered" (1 Pet. 3:7). Here he intimates that discord in families tends to hinder Christians in their prayers. And what Christian that has made the sad experiment, has not done it to his sorrow, and in his own experience does not bear witness to the truth of the apostle's intimation?

Why contention has this effect of hindering spiritual exercises and comforts and hopes, and of destroying the sweet hope of that which is heavenly, we may learn from the doctrine we have considered. For heaven being a world of love, it follows that, when we have the least exercise of love, and the most of a contrary spirit, then we have the least of heaven, and are farthest from it in the frame of our mind. Then we have the least of the exercise of that wherein consists a conformity to heaven, and a preparation for it, and what tends to it; and so, necessarily, we must have least evidence of our title to heaven, and be farthest from the comfort which such evidence affords. . . .

[2. *How happy are those who are entitled to heaven.*]

3. *What has been said on this subject may well awaken and alarm sinners.* Here I will consider two points.

First, by putting them in mind of their misery, in that they have no portion or right in this world of love. You have heard what has been said of heaven, what kind of glory and blessedness is there, and how happy the saints and angels are in that world of perfect love. But consider that none of this belongs to you. When you hear of such things, you hear of that in which you have no interest. No such person as you, a wicked hater of God and Christ and one that is under the power of a spirit of enmity against all that is good, shall ever enter there. Such as you never belong to the faithful Israel of God, and shall never enter their heavenly rest. It may be said to you, as Peter said to Simon, "Thou hast neither part nor lot in this matter: for thy heart is not right in the sight of God" (Acts 8:21). And it may be said to you, as Nehemiah said to Sanballat and his associates, "You have no portion, nor right, nor memorial, in Jerusalem" (Neh. 2:20). . . .

Second, by showing sinners that they are in danger. Hell is a world of hatred. There are three worlds. One is this, which is an intermediate world, a world in which good and evil are so mixed together as to be a sure sign that this world is not to continue forever. Another is heaven, a world of love, without any hatred. And the other is hell, a world of hatred, where there is no love, which is the world to which all of you who are in a

Christless state properly belong. This last is the world where God manifests his displeasure and wrath, as in heaven he manifests his love. Everything in hell is hateful. There is not one solitary object there that is not odious and detestable, horrid and hateful. There is no person or thing to be seen there, that is amiable or lovely; nothing that is pure, or holy, or pleasant, but everything abominable and odious. There are no beings there but devils, and damned spirits that are like devils. Hell is, as it were, a vast den of poisonous hissing serpents; the old serpent, who is the devil and Satan, and with him all his hateful brood. In that dark world there are none but those whom God hates with a perfect and everlasting hatred. He exercises no love, and extends no mercy to any one object there, but pours out upon them horrors without mixture. . . .

Now consider, all you that are out of Christ, and that were never born again, and that never had any blessed renovation of your hearts by the Holy Spirit implanting divine love in them, and leading you to choose the happiness that consists in holy love as your best and sweetest good, and to spend your life in struggling after holiness. Consider your danger, and what is before you. For this is the world to which you are condemned; the world to which you belong through the sentence of the law; the world that every day and hour you are in danger of having your abode everlastingly fixed in; and the world to which, if you repent not, you will soon go, instead of going to that blessed world of love of which you have now heard. Consider that it is indeed thus with you. These things are not cunningly devised fables, but the great and dreadful realities of God's Word, and things that, in a little while, you will know with everlasting certainty are true. How, then, can you rest in such a state as you are in, and go about so carelessly from day to day, and so heedless and negligent of your precious, immortal souls? . . .

4. *Let the consideration of what has been said of heaven stir up all earnestly to seek after it.* If heaven be such a blessed world, then let it be our chosen country, and the inheritance that we look for and seek. Let us turn our course this way, and press on to its possession. It is not impossible but that this glorious world may be obtained by us. It is offered to us. Though it be so excellent and blessed a country, yet God stands ready to give us an inheritance there, if it be but the country that we desire, and will choose, and diligently seek. God gives us our choice. We may have our inheritance wherever we choose it, and may obtain heaven if we will but seek it by patient continuance in well-doing. . . .

And for direction on how to seek heaven,

First, let not your heart go after the things of this world, as your chief good. Indulge not yourself in the possession of earthly things as though they were to satisfy your soul. . . . You must mortify the desires of vain-glory, and become poor in spirit and lowly in heart.

Second, you must, in your meditations and holy exercises, be much engaged in conversing with heavenly persons, and objects, and enjoyments. You cannot constantly be seeking heaven, without having your thoughts much there. . . . Think often of all that is in heaven, of the friends who are there, and the praises and worship there, and of all that will make up the blessedness of that world of love. Let your conversation be in heaven (Phil 3:20).

Third, be content to pass through all difficulties in the way to heaven. Though the path is before you, and you may walk in it if you desire, yet it is a way that is ascending, and filled with many difficulties and obstacles. That glorious city of light and love is, as it were, on the top of a high hill or mountain, and there is no way to it but by upward and arduous steps. But though the ascent be difficult, and the way full of trials, still it is worth your while to meet them all for the sake of coming and dwelling in such a glorious city at last. . . . At every step it will be easier and easier to ascend; and the higher your ascent, the more will you be cheered by the glorious prospect before you, and by a nearer view of that heavenly city where in a little while you shall forever be at rest.

Fourth, in all your way let your eye be fixed on Jesus, who has gone to heaven as your forerunner. Look to him. Behold his glory in heaven, for a sight of it may stir you up the more earnestly to desire to be there. . . . Look to him as your mediator, and trust in the atonement which he has made, entering into the holiest of all in the upper temple. Look to him as your intercessor, who forever pleads for you before the throne of God. Look to him as your strength, that by his Spirit he may enable you to press on, and overcome every difficulty of the way. Trust in his promises of heaven to those that love and follow him, which he has confirmed by entering into heaven as the head, and representative, and Savior of his people.

Fifth, if you would be in the way to the world of love, see that you live a life of love, of love to God, and love to men. All of us hope to have part in the world of love hereafter, and therefore we should cherish the spirit of love, and live a life of holy love here on earth. This is the way to be like the inhabitants of heaven, who are now confirmed in love forever. Only in this way can you be like them in excellence and loveliness, and like them, too, in happiness, and rest, and joy. By living in love in this world you may be like them, too, in sweet and holy peace, and thus have, on earth, the foretastes of heavenly pleasures and delights.

Thus, also, you may have a sense of the glory of heavenly things, as of God, and Christ, and holiness; and your heart be disposed and opened by holy love to God, and by the spirit of peace and love to men, to a sense of the excellence and sweetness of all that is to be found in heaven. Thus shall the windows of heaven be as it were opened, so that its glorious light shall shine in upon your soul. Thus you may have the evidence of your fitness for that blessed world, and that you are actually on the way to its possession. And being thus made fit, through grace, for the inheritance of the saints in light, when a few more days shall have passed away, you shall be with them in their blessedness forever. Happy, three times happy are those who shall thus be found faithful to the end, and then shall be welcomed to the joy of their Lord! There "they shall hunger no more, neither thirst any more; neither shall the sun light on them, nor any heat. For the Lamb which is in the midst of the throne shall feed them, and lead them to living fountains of waters: and God shall wipe away all tears from their eyes" (Rev. 7:16-17).

By living a life of love, you will be in the way to heaven. *As heaven is a world of love, so the way to heaven is the way of love.* This will best prepare you for heaven, and prepare you for an inheritance with the saints in the land of light and love. And if ever you arrive at heaven, faith and love must be the wings which must carry you there.

NOTES

CHAPTER ONE: LIVING IN BETWEEN

1. Dietrich Bonhoeffer to Eberhard Bethge, June 27, 1944, in *Letters and Papers from Prison* (New York: Simon & Schuster, 1997), 336-337.

2. For a fuller sketch of the life of Jonathan Edwards, see Stephen J. Nichols, *Jonathan Edwards: A Guided Tour of His Life and Thought* (Phillipsburg, NJ: P&R, 2001) and the essays in John Piper and Justin Taylor, editors, *A God-Entranced Vision of All Things: The Legacy of Jonathan Edwards* (Wheaton, IL: Crossway Books, 2004).

CHAPTER TWO: ON THE WAY TO HEAVEN

1. For this sermon, and the sermon series that it concludes, see Jonathan Edwards, *Charity and Its Fruits*, ed. Tryon Edwards, 1851, reprinted by Banner of Truth, 1969. The sermon may also be found in *The Works of Jonathan Edwards, Volume 8: Ethical Writings*, ed. Paul Ramsey (New Haven, CT: Yale University Press, 1989), 366-397.

2. Cornelius Plantinga, *Not the Way It's Supposed to Be: A Breviary of Sin* (Grand Rapids, MI: Eerdmans, 1995).

3. See John Milton, *Paradise Lost*, Books IX and X.

4. Raoul Wallenberg (1912-?). Much mystery surrounds the final event and the death of Wallenberg. He was captured by Russian forces, but beyond that little is known of what became of him. I am grateful to Dale Mort for making me aware of Wallenberg's example.

CHAPTER THREE: BEING GOOD CITIZENS

1. For further discussion of this in New Testament scholarship, see M. Reasoner, "Citizenship, Roman and Heavenly," in *Dictionary of Paul and His Letters*, ed. Gerald F. Hawthorne and Ralph P. Martin (Downers Grove, IL: InterVarsity Press, 1993), 139-141.

2. Gordon Fee, *Paul's Letter to the Philippians* (Grand Rapids, MI: Eerdmans, 1995), 378.

3. The sermon is reprinted in *The Sermons of Jonathan Edwards: A Reader*, ed. Wilson H. Kimnach, Kenneth P. Minkema, and Douglas A. Sweeney (New Haven, CT: Yale University Press, 1999), 13-25. For more on Edwards in New York, see George M. Marsden, *Jonathan Edwards: A Life* (New Haven, CT: Yale University Press, 2003).

4. See John Piper, *God Is the Gospel: Meditations on God's Love as the Gift of Himself* (Wheaton, IL: Crossway, 2005), esp. 133-145.
5. William Shakespeare, *The Tragedy of Hamlet, Prince of Denmark*, Act I, Scene 2.
6. Wendell Berry, "Manifesto: The Mad Farmer Liberation Front," *The Country of Marriage* (New York: Harcourt Brace Jovanovich, 1973).
7. Jeremiah Burroughs, *Hope* (Orlando, FL: Soli Deo Gloria, 2005), 2.

CHAPTER FOUR: BUT TO ACT JUSTLY

1. See Richard Gott, *Cuba: A New History* (New Haven, CT: Yale University Press, 2004), 13-15. The account was originally recorded by Bartolome de Las Casas, a priest who accompanied Velasquez, in *A Short History of the Destruction of the Indies* (1542).
2. The sermon "Much in Deeds of Charity" may be found in *The Sermons of Jonathan Edwards: A Reader*, ed. Wilson H. Kimnach, Kenneth P. Minkema, and Douglas A. Sweeney (New Haven, CT: Yale University Press, 1999), 197-211.
3. Carl F. H. Henry, *The Uneasy Conscience of Modern Fundamentalism* (Grand Rapids, MI: Eerdmans, 2003, first published 1947), 2.
4. The sermon "Christian Charity, or The Duty of Charity to the Poor: Explained and Enforced" may be found in *The Works of Jonathan Edwards, Volume Two*, ed. Edward Hickman (Carlisle, PA: The Banner of Truth, 1974), 163-173.
5. C. S. Lewis, *The Weight of Glory* (New York: Harper San Francisco, 2001), 45-46.
6. For a fuller treatment of Edwards at Stockbridge, see Stephen J. Nichols, "Last of the Mohican Missionaries: Jonathan Edwards at Stockbridge," in *The Legacy of Jonathan Edwards: American Religion and the Evangelical Tradition*, ed. D. G. Hart, Sean Michael Lucas, and Stephen J. Nichols (Grand Rapids, MI: Baker Academic, 2003), 47-63.
7. Jonathan Edwards to Joseph Paice, in *The Works of Jonathan Edwards: Volume 16, Letters and Personal Writings*, ed. George S. Claghorn (New Haven, CT: Yale University Press, 1998), 437.
8. John M. Perkins, *Let Justice Roll Down* (Ventura, CA: Regal Books, 1976).

CHAPTER FIVE: WHILE WE WAIT

1. The sermon "I Know My Redeemer Lives" may be found in *The Sermons of Jonathan Edwards: A Reader*, ed. Wilson H. Kimnach, Kenneth P. Minkema, and Douglas A. Sweeney (New Haven, CT: Yale University Press, 1999), 141-160.

2. The sermon "The Peace Which Christ Gives His True Followers" may be found in *The Works of Jonathan Edwards, Volume Two*, ed. Edward Hickman (Carlisle, PA: The Banner of Truth, 1974), 89-93.

3. For more discussion of Edwards's dismissal from Northampton, see Stephen J. Nichols, *Jonathan Edwards: A Guided Tour of His Life and Thought* (Phillipsburg, NJ: P&R, 2001), 125-137.

4. Heidi L. Nichols, *Anne Bradstreet: A Guided Tour of the Life and Thought of a Puritan Poet* (Philipsburg, NJ: P&R, 2006), 195-197.

5. I am grateful to Stephen Heitland, one of my students, for pointing this out to me.

CHAPTER SIX: IT'S ONLY THE BEGINNING

1. The word translated "mansions" in the King James Version is *mone* in the Greek. It literally means "dwelling places," being related to the verb *meno*, "to abide." The KJV translators were unduly influenced by the Latin Vulgate text, which uses the word *mansiones*. In this context, with the reference to the house of God, it is best translated "many rooms," as in the English Standard Version. The idea is dwelling together in the Father's house, not row after row of Beverly Hills mansions. See D. A. Carson, *The Gospel According to John* (Grand Rapids, MI: Eerdmans, 1991), 488-490.

2. Edwards's sermon "Many Mansions," preached on Christmas Day 1737, may be found in *The Works of Jonathan Edwards, Volume 19: Sermons and Discourses, 1734-1738*, ed. M. X. Lesser (New Haven, CT: Yale University Press, 2001), 734-746.

3. These citations are from Edwards's sermon on Revelation 14:2, a "Thanksgiving Sermon," preached on November 7, 1734. It may be found in *The Works of Jonathan Edwards, Volume Two*, ed. Edward Hickman (Carlisle, PA: The Banner of Truth, 1974), 913-917.

4. The sermon "Serving God in Heaven" may be found in *The Works of Jonathan Edwards: Volume 17, Sermons and Discourses, 1730-1733*, ed. Mark Valeri (New Haven, CT: Yale University Press, 1999), 253-261.

5. For a recent treatment on humility, well-seasoned with references to Edwards, see C. J. Mahaney, *Humility: True Greatness* (Sisters, OR: Multnomah, 2005).

CHAPTER SEVEN: MEETING THERE AT LAST

1. For this letter, see *The Works of Jonathan Edwards: Volume 16, Letters and Personal Writings*, ed. George S. Claghorn (New Haven, CT: Yale University Press, 1998), 576-578.

2. For the account of his death and for the family's correspondence on the

occasion, see *The Works of Jonathan Edwards, Volume One*, ed. Edward Hickman (Carlisle, PA: Banner of Truth, 1974), clxxviii-clxxx.

3. For more on Sarah Edwards, see Heidi L. Nichols, "Those Exceptional Edwards Women," *Christian History* 22 (2003): 23-25 and Noël Piper, "Sarah Edwards: Jonathan's Home and Haven," *A God-Entranced Vision of All Things: The Legacy of Jonathan Edwards*, ed. John Piper and Justin Taylor (Wheaton, IL: Crossway Books, 2004), 55-78.

4. Martin Luther, *Luther's Works, Volume 54: Table Talk* (Philadelphia: Fortress Press, 1967), 432.

5. The sermon may be found in *The Works of Jonathan Edwards, Volume Two*, ed. Edward Hickman (Carlisle, PA: The Banner of Truth, 1974), 965-969.

6. The sermon "The Christian Pilgrim; Or, The True Christian's Life a Journey Toward Heaven" may be found in *The Works of Jonathan Edwards, Volume Two*, ed. Edward Hickman (Carlisle, PA: The Banner of Truth, 1974), 243-246.

7. Jonathan Edwards, sermon manuscript on Hebrews 11:16 (January 1754), Beinecke Library, Yale University.

APPENDIX: "HEAVEN IS A WORLD OF LOVE" BY JONATHAN EDWARDS

1. Edwards is referring to the previous sermon in the series. The full doctrine for that sermon, based on 1 Corinthians 13:8, reads, "That great fruit of the Spirit in which the Holy Ghost shall not only for a season but everlastingly be communicated to the church of Christ is divine love."